STRATEGY
MATTERS

STRATEGY MATTERS

A SIMPLE 7-STEP PROCESS TO GO FROM STRUGGLE TO SUCCESS

ROBERT M. STOVER

TIMBER COVE PRESS

Robert Stover © 2010

WARNINGS AND DISCLAIMERS

This book is designed to provide information on strategy and strategic planning. It is sold with the understanding that the publisher and author are not engaged in rendering legal, accounting or other professional services. If legal or other expert assistances is required, the services of a competent professional should be sought.

It is not the purpose of this manual to represent all the information otherwise available to businesses on strategy and strategic planning. You are urged to read all the available material, learn as much as possible about strategy and strategic planning and tailor the information to your individual needs.

Neither strategy nor strategic planning are guarantees of success. While strategic planning may increase your probabilities, no guarantee of success is possible.

Every effort has been made to make this manual as complete and accurate as possible. However, there may be mistakes, both typographical and in content. Therefore, this text should be used only as a general guide and not as the ultimate source of strategy and strategic planning information. Furthermore, this manual contains information on strategic planning that is current only up to the printing date.

The purpose of this manual is to educate and inform. The author and Timber Cove Press shall have neither liability nor responsibility to any person or entity with respect to any loss or damage caused, or alleged to have been caused, directly or indirectly, by the information contained in this book.

If you do not wish to be bound by the above, you may return this book to the publisher for a full refund.

ISBN-10: 098-3-0278-0-3
ISBN-13: 978-0-9830278-0-5

Library of Congress Control Number: 2010938686

Book Design by DesignForBooks.com
Cover photo credit ©iStockphoto/urbancow

To Laura

Your fingerprints are on this book . . .

. . . and my heart

Contents

Preface **vii**

Introduction **ix**

1. The Magic of Strategy **1**

2. Where Are You? **11**

3. Vision: Where Are You Going? **33**

4. Obstacles: What's in Your Way? **53**

5. Resources: The Art of Resourcefulness **57**

6. Strategy: How Will You Get There? **73**

7. Tactics: Who's Doing What by When? **87**

8. Monitor: How Are We Doing? **95**

Notes **105**

Bibliography **107**

Acknowledgements **111**

Index **113**

About the Author **119**

Preface

The 48 Million Dollar Difference

Two entrepreneurs I know both started businesses in the same industry. Both worked 15-hour days. Both were committed to their visions.

Three years later . . .

Both have battle scars. Both have made mistakes. Both have overcome obstacles that would stagger most of us.

One sells his company for $48 million.

The other continues to struggle.

The difference?

Strategy.

Introduction

As a business leader, there is a powerful force waiting to help you achieve your dreams for your business. This force can catapult sales, multiply profits, and accelerate growth. It can give you an unfair advantage over competitors. And it can bring a deeply satisfying purpose and direction to both you and your team.

What is this force?

Strategy.

And this book will give you a simple, step-by-step formula that lets you harness this power and put it to work in your business.

Sadly, I find many businesses shy away from strategic planning because it's been made too complex, dry, and time-consuming.

*Strategy Is Power
It's the power to
outwit, outsmart,
and outflank
stronger competi-
tors.*

As a business leader fighting the daily battles for cash flow, sales, and profits, the last thing you need is a book loaded with complex formulas, analyses, and spreadsheets placed in your hands. What you need is a simple formula that helps you think more strategically—quickly and easily.

Look, the payoffs of a little strategic thinking about your business can make such a large impact on your profits and future I'd rather you spend a half hour with a napkin at lunch with your key managers than keep putting off a rigorous six-month strategic analysis.

Here's why . . .

IT'S MORE POWERFUL
THAN MONEY

During the last Internet boom we saw hundreds of dotcoms that were swimming in an ocean of cash, blow it all and go bankrupt. They had money. They needed strategy.

STRATEGY IS POWER

It's the power to outwit, outsmart, and outflank stronger competitors. It's the power to multiply every dollar, every hour, and every drop of sweat you invest in your business. It's the power to achieve your dreams for the business faster—much faster.

As you turn through these pages you'll see how strategy can make your marketing, advertising, and promotional investments pull up to three times more results. That means your competitors would have to spend 300% more on their marketing budget just to keep even with you.

Conversely, it means you could produce the same results you are getting today for a fraction of the time, effort, and money you are expending right now.

And you'll discover that strategic breakthroughs often mean that you spend less time, money, and effort to create greater results than you're achieving now.

STRATEGY UNLOCKS WEALTH

Many business leaders were shocked at how much pent-up wealth was within their grasp—once they created a breakthrough strategy.

STRATEGY LETS THE
WEAK OVERCOME THE STRONG

Strategy allows the weak to overcome the strong. Strategy multiplies your resources. Strategy protects against attacks. Strategy brings stability.

Failure on your part to shape and craft your own strategy means that competitors and market forces will do the job for you.

HERE'S THE BAD NEWS

Here's the bad news: This force can also be used by your competitors.

Failure on your part to shape and craft your own strategy means that competitors and market forces will do the job for you.

Taking this passive approach to strategy means you're like a ping-pong ball on a storm-tossed sea: blown here and there at the will of forces you don't control. And in the case of your competitors— by forces bent on your destruction.

Here's the bottom line: Right now, good or bad, you have a strategy. The strategy you have is creating the results you're getting now. Want to change your results? Then you need to change your strategy.

So, with all the potential of strategy to help you achieve your dreams for the business, doesn't it make sense to spend a while thinking about how to put this powerful ally to work more effectively in your business?

Turn the page and let's do that now . . .

1

The Magic of Strategy

In the year 756 BC, Chinese general Zhang Xun had a problem. His city was besieged by a stronger enemy, and his men were out of arrows.

What to do? Surrender?

Zhang Xun ordered that 1,000 straw men be made and dressed in black clothes. That night he had the straw men lowered over the city walls mimicking a raid on the enemy. And the enemy responded by showering tens of thousands of arrows on the raiders. After the shower of arrows stopped, Zhang had the straw men pulled back over the walls, thus replenishing his own supply of arrows while simultaneously depleting the enemy's.

The next night Zhang Xun ordered the straw men lowered back over the walls. But the enemy was not fooled a second time by the trick and shot no arrows.

Surprisingly, Zhang Xun again ordered men lowered over the walls a third night. Again, the enemy was not fooled. But what they didn't realize was that the wise general had ordered real soldiers lowered over the walls. The soldiers, when safely on the ground, launched a surprise attack and routed the enemy.

That story illustrates the magic of strategy.

THE MAGIC OF STRATEGY

Strategy is the art of achieving your goals, objectives, and visions with the resources at hand.

The magic of strategy is its ability to help you achieve results far out of proportion with your seeming resources. And it's that power that this book aims to give you in an easy, step-by-step process.

You see, strategy is too important to the future of your business to be made difficult.

Using the approach here, you or your managers can think strategically about issues in an hour or less. Or, you can expand the process to be used in a 1–3-day strategy retreat.

Because of the importance of strategy to the future of a business, strategic planning has taken on a thoroughness bordering on paranoia. Some companies take a year or longer just to create a plan.

And while detail and complexity are admirable, they will get the average business killed in today's chaotic, fast-moving markets.

I've worked with clients in markets so turbulent that the competitors, customer demands, and market landscape are radically altered in just 6 months.

CATAPULT YOUR BUSINESS TO THE NEXT LEVEL

So, this book was written with a belief in the power of strategy and strategic planning to catapult your business to the next level, but also with a clear eye on reality. If a planning process takes too much time and is too complex, it's either not going to get done—or be irrelevant by the time it's finished.

> *You need a strategic planning process that is simple, but not simplistic. Thorough, but not complex.*

In today's world, you need a strategic planning process that is simple, but not simplistic. Thorough, but not complex.

On the other hand, limited time, the urgencies of the day, and uncertain futures are not excuses to avoid strategic thinking. You must make time for strategic thinking. Your future success depends on it.

It's a fact of life that none of us (not you, not me, not billionaires, not multi-billion dollar corporations) have all the resources we need to achieve our respective visions for the future.

So, we need a magic wand to multiply our resources.

Strategy is that wand.

And the magic behind all strategy is "concentration." Strategy focuses our minds on a clear, compelling vision of the future, and then concentrates our thinking, resources, and efforts on those critical few actions that will make the biggest impact.

While strategic thinking has a reputation as being an analytical, dry process, you'll discover that by creating a tension between your vision and your resources, strategic thinking makes room for the imagination to do its magical work.

Here's a quick overview of the simple, seven-step process we will use to unleash this imagination, power, and magic in your business.

STEP 1

WHERE ARE YOU NOW?

In this section we take a look at the two major drivers of strategic planning: stuff that is happening now, and stuff we think is about to happen to our business.

That can be good stuff, but it's usually bad stuff.

Nothing happens until you have a vision.

So, in Step One we get clear on the problems, challenges, and future dangers facing your business. Then we narrow them down to those that will create the most impact.

STEP 2
WHAT'S THE VISION?

While problems and challenges drive the need for strategic thinking, it is vision that drives the rest of the strategy process.

Nothing happens until you have a vision. The more clear and compelling your vision, the more powerful and imaginative your strategy will be.

The vision you craft in this step will act as the "North Star" to the rest of your strategic planning process.

STEP 3
WHAT ARE THE OBSTACLES?

To have a vision is to have obstacles. They appear the minute your vision is formed.

Yet, many business leaders have trouble taking a realist's perspective and looking big obstacles squarely in the eye.

Looking at and admitting major obstacles to your vision does not make you a pessimist. The purpose of looking at obstacles is not to look for excuses and reasons not to pursue the vision. It's to look at what our strategy must overcome, so that it can be as effective as possible.

Failure to look at obstacles and adapt your strategy to them creates nasty surprises.

Looking at big scary obstacles realistically gives the imagination the fuel it needs to craft innovative strategies for victory.

STEP 4

WHAT ARE OUR RESOURCES?

Only after you know what the dangers are, what your vision for the future is, and what's standing in the way are we ready to look at our resources.

We are looking for two major elements: what resources we have to help us achieve our vision, and what resources we need.

Why not do this first—before vision? Won't a vision be more realistic if we first look to resources?

The truth is a resource often isn't a resource until a vision gives it meaning and use.

A rock at my campsite isn't a resource until I discover I forgot a hammer to pound on the tent stakes—or a bear is threatening my life.

In the same way, you've got "rocks" lying around your business that you would never think to use until a compelling vision gives them meaning as a resource.

STEP 5
WHAT'S OUR STRATEGY?

Strategy exists to serve your vision.

Vision and Resources answer the questions, "Where do we want to go?" and "Where are we now?" Strategy answers the question, "How do we get there?"

During this step you'll take a look at your resources, mix in some imagination, and create a path around, under, or over your obstacles to take you to your vision in the fastest way possible.

STEP 6
WHAT ARE OUR TACTICS?

Now that we know our major strategic direction, it's time to get specific with details, timetables, and accountabilities.

Tactics answer the question, "Who's going to do what by when?"

Ironically, if you, or a member of your team, excels at vision and imagination, this will be the toughest step.

On the other hand, if you are a realist and know all that "dreaming" won't make anything happen, this will be your favorite step.

Either way, nothing will happen until you complete this step in the strategic-thinking process.

It's time to make something happen!

STEP 7
WHAT WILL WE
MONITOR AND MEASURE?

In the late 1800s, famed military strategist Field Marshall Helmuth Carl Bernard von Moltke noted, "No battle plan survives contact with the enemy."

What's interesting is that this quote was from a military man who was known to take thousands of variables into account when crafting his battle plan.

Things change. You had better adapt to them.

His point being: Things change. You had better adapt to them.

Vision is about the future, and strategy is about how to get there. Yet, no man knows the future—and no amount of intense data gathering will ever fully reveal the future.

Therefore we need to constantly monitor our strategy and tactics, making adjustments where necessary to keep us driving toward our vision.

Too often I see business leaders get so locked on a specific strategy or tactic that they fail to realize when it is time to try something different.

Monitoring and measuring the right things is the only way to keep you on track and on time.

IT'S YOUR FUTURE

Neither you nor I can predict what will happen in the future. But we've been given the amazing ability to shape it in ways no one else can imagine.

As Dandridge Cole once said, "We cannot predict the future, but we can invent it."

This simple, seven-step process will help you move from today's challenges and frustrations to a richer future.

And whether you want to use this process for yourself, or for a full-blown strategy retreat with your team, you'll find additional resources and templates online at *www. strategymatters.com/book*

Now, let's turn the page and take the first step on our journey to a better future . . .

2

Where Are You?

One of the classic texts on strategy is The Art of War by Sun Tzu. In it he wrote words that the business leader should take to heart today . . .

"Know the enemy and know yourself, you need not fear the result of a hundred battles. If you know yourself but not the enemy, for every victory gained you will also suffer a defeat. If you know neither the enemy nor yourself, you will succumb in every battle."[1]

At almost the same time in history as Sun Tzu, Socrates noted "The unexamined life is not worth living."

2400 years later, Mark Twain responded with a comeback, "The unexamined life may not be worth living, but the life too closely examined may not be lived at all."

The unexamined business may not be worth running, but a business too closely examined never gets run at all.

What's true in life, is true in business. The unexamined business may not be worth running, but a business too closely examined never gets run at all.

Too often I see businesses that have not formally examined their problems, opportunities, customers, competitors, and competencies. They don't have a clear idea of "Where are we at now?" As a result, these enterprises only reach a fraction of their potential.

Worse, dangers get overlooked or swept under the rug, and opportunities are left for competitors to exploit.

Just as dangerously, we all know business leaders who can never seem to collect enough data or do enough analysis to make a decision about the direction of their business.

Either way, the result is the same. They get run over on the business super-highway. They are forced to watch others achieve prosperity with opportunities that should have been theirs.

So, as a business leader, you must examine your business to know where you are now—today. This is the starting point of your strategy. Yet, you must do it within a reasonable amount of time. And in today's environment—faster is better.

AVOID FIXATION

Years ago I had the opportunity to take emergency medical training and learned a principle I think is critical for anyone doing strategic planning to consider.

We were taught the danger of fixating too quickly on the big, obvious injury.

You see, it's human nature for a rescuer to approach an accident victim, see blood coming out of their forehead and fixate all their efforts immediately on that big, obvious problem.

But what a rescuer may not realize is that the reason the victim is bleeding from the forehead is they had a seizure, fell, and not only cut their head on the sharp edge of a table, but broke their neck as well.

By fixating on the obvious injury, the rescuer could easily do far more damage than good to the accident victim.

So, they are taught to do a "primary survey," a quick scan of the entire body that looks beyond the obvious to other, more threatening injuries.

THE FAST SCAN FORMULA

In this chapter, you'll learn to do a primary survey, called a FAST SCAN, to check all your business's vital signs and expose unseen problems or opportunities.

Here's what we are going to take a look at:

F. **Frustrations**
A. **Adversaries**
S. **Segments**
T. **Trends**

S. **Sums**
C. **Competencies**
A. **Assumptions**
N. **N-Joy**

The purpose of the FAST SCAN is to step back and take a broad view of your entire business, its markets, its problems, and its opportunities. During the first part of the scan, the goal is to list as many issues as you can. Then, during the second part of the scan, you will narrow those issues down to the critical few that you believe will have the most impact on your business going forward into the future.

Our FAST SCAN will begin where most strategic planning begins: frustrations with the way things are.

FRUSTRATIONS

In theory, strategic planning is driven by a blend of both problems and opportunities. But in reality, 90% of business leaders who are exploring strategic thinking are facing a major frustration or problem.

The good news is that problems and frustrations are often the seeds of great business achievements. In fact, most of the innovation in the world is initially inspired by someone getting frustrated and fed up enough to finally solve a problem in a new way.

In the same way, your current problems and frustrations with the business can be used as the catapult that takes your business to the next level.

> *Problems and frustrations are often the seeds of great business achievements.*

Many business leaders are born optimists. They cringe at the idea of spending time focusing on problems. Seemingly, even worse is letting team members voice their issues; it's seen as "whining," "negativity," "unproductive thinking," and "bad for morale."

The truth is that problems left to metastasize are like a cancer in an organization. Suppressing their expression only creates much bigger problems in the future.

So, if you're leading a strategy session, or doing one on your own, begin by listing all the problems and frustrations the business is feeling. What's going on in sales? Marketing? HR? Finance? Operations? IT?

List all the problems, frustrations, concerns, and challenges you and your team can generate in this step.

ADVERSARIES

The basic premise of business seems so easy: Find a need and fill it.

But, then along come competitive adversaries who look at the customers you serve and try to serve them better, faster, and cheaper.

In looking at our competitors, we always have an eye on their strengths and weaknesses. We want to avoid the former and exploit the latter.

Write out who your most dangerous competitors are in the market and then take stock of them.

What is their growth rate compared to yours? Their profitability? Their operating costs?

What are their strengths? What customer segments are they strongest with? Weakest? When you compete head-to-head for customers, why do they win? What customer segments do you win most with? Why? What implications does this have for your strategy?

Are your competitors exploiting mediums, channels, or technologies that you are not?

How are they positioned in the market?

If you were your competitor, how would you beat your company?

Do their weaknesses point to opportunities to better serve customers?

Three Critical Questions
Your Strategy Must Answer

Your business strategy comes out of three primary decisions—Whom you target as customers. What you offer them. How you approach them.

But you don't make these decisions in isolation. You must consider competition. This is an illustration of head-to-head competition. You are offering the same customers the same thing in the same way as the competition does. Unless you are the big dog in the market, probably not a good idea.

So, you can beat the competition by offering your customers something different, approaching them in a new way—or both.

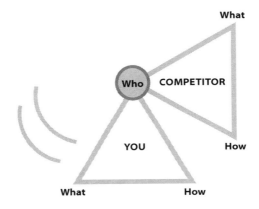

Or, you can find a new segment of the market to target where you are not competing for the same customers.

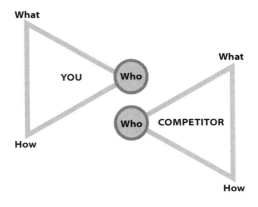

After taking a good hard (and honest) look at your toughest competitors, it's time to step back and look at more non-traditional adversaries.

Are there new technologies that threaten to replace your product or service offerings? Are there substitutes for how you and your competitors serve customers?

Remember that CD manufacturers were watching each other. But it was MP3s that took the biggest bite out of their market.

SEGMENTS

Next to profit, the biggest purpose of a business is to serve customers. So, here we take a look at your customers and the major segments they fall into.

It is critical that you move beyond thinking of customers generically and begin thinking of them in segments.

Why?

Three reasons:

One, not all customers are created equal.

Some customers are far more valuable to the future of your business than others.

In fact, your choice of customer segments is one of the most important decisions you make in crafting a strategy.

Two, major growth and innovation come from thinking about your customer segments in fresh ways.

Some customers are far more valuable to the future of your business than others.

Three, markets tend to break into smaller and smaller segments as competitors look for ways to win. You need to be aware of how your market is breaking up—and how your competitors may be winning in these new segments.

So, in this step of the scan you list your major customer segments and analyze which are most valuable to your business.

There are hundreds of ways to segment your customers. Here's a few to get you started thinking.

Demographics

Demographics are usually hard facts. You can often put a number on them.

To target consumers, you may look at the age of your customers, their social class, their household incomes, religious affiliation, race, sex, number of cars they own, size of their families, and many other factors.

On the other hand, if you target businesses, consider: yearly revenue of the business, number of employees, position within a company, industry, service or manufacturing or technology businesses, annual growth rate, privately owned or not, and others.

Geographics

Geographics are straightforward. It's the "Where?" of your customers. Are they local, within a county, state, nation, or global?

Psychographics

Psychographics are the soft factors encompassing lifestyle choices, values, and beliefs. Some segments are adventurous, other cautious. Some purchase to make a statement.

For example, as I write this now, many consumers are making purchases to bolster their beliefs and make statements about being "green." And, just as importantly, there is a growing "anti-green" movement.

Behavioral

Behavioral factors include heavy users, non-users, frequency of purchase, size of purchase, purchase amount in dollars, and recency of purchase.

Utility

Utility encompasses the end result: "Why?" customers actually make the purchase.

If you're a B2B company, then sales, profits, waste elimination, cost savings, time savings, sales growth, lead generation, competitive advantage, and efficiency may be your utility segments.

It is eye-opening how many new opportunities for growth, product development, and competitive advantage emerge.

For a master's course in segmentation, take a look at the toothpaste aisle in the grocery or drug store.

There are toothpastes targeted at kids, older adults, people with sensitive teeth, people who smoke, people who want whiter teeth, fresher breath, plaque prevention, total care, and folks who want a natural toothpaste, flavors such as orange, cinnamon, and mint, and there are travel, single, small family, and big family sizes.

It's truly amazing to look at the number of segments encompassing demographics, psychographics, and utility that toothpaste manufacturers have both discovered and created.

In strategy sessions I've run at companies, it is eye-opening how many new opportunities for growth, product development, and competitive advantage emerge from a systematic look at the possible segments available to a company.

So, which customer segments are the most profitable? Which are growing the fastest? Which are shrinking? Which are most competitive? Which have competitors overlooked?

TRENDS

According to Newton's laws of motion, an object in motion stays in motion unless acted upon by an equal or greater force. The same is true of the major trends in the world around us. Trends are like the weather, and can either buffet or help your business sail into the future.

Obviously, we can't know the future, but it is wise to have an eye on major trends in the world around your business.

Let's step back and take a broad look around us . . .

What major trends are happening in our markets, our country, with government? Are these likely to keep growing into the foreseeable future?

What's happening economically? Upturns? Downturns? Embargos? Trade restrictions?

Is the government moving toward tighter regulations and control—or deregulation?

What's going on politically? Are things moving in a more liberal or more conservative direction? Is there a period of strife and instability?

What major technologies are emerging? The last decade it was the Internet. This decade?

What's the mood of people in the markets and countries you operate in? Optimistic? Pessimistic? Frightened?

And one of the most predictable trends to keep an eye on is major demographics. Is the population aging? Getting younger? Is one or another ethnic group rising in numbers and influence? Declining?

SUMS

Results are not always equal to the efforts expended.

Sums and measurements are like a searchlight: They shine into the fog of opinion and conjecture and bring clarity to the path one should take.

Time and again I've seen a simple 80/20 analysis on the most profitable customer segments or the most profitable products change the direction and fortune of companies.

So often we get mired in day-to-day firefighting and problem-solving that we lose site of our businesses' key vital signs.

It is not at all unusual for a business leader to discover that the area that gets the most attention, the most talent, and the most funding is getting beat by the product or customer segment that no one is paying attention to.

Results are not always equal to the efforts expended. And, unless you measure, your team assumes that where they are working the hardest they are producing the greatest results.

Here are some general suggestions on sums and numbers that may help you know where you are now.

General	Financial	Customer
• Cash flow • Balance sheet • Income statements • Profitability by customer and product	• EBITA • Net profit after tax • Return on capital • Revenue per employee	• Number of customers • Average order size • Frequency of purchase • Lifetime value • Most-profitable customers

Marketing	Sales	Customer service
• Market share • Segment growth	• Best/worst performing representative • Sales per rep. • Calls per rep. • Profitability per rep.	• Percent of returns to sales • Time until order fulfilled • Number of complaints

The bottom line is that there are many measures that can be used to take the pulse of your business; so you need to use common sense and choose the measures that are most critical to the operation of your business given the opportunities and challenges facing you.

COMPETENCIES

Following Sun Tzu's earlier advice, it is now time to "know ourselves."

In this portion of the scan, we want to zero in on what makes us unique from competitors at a core level. What unique, core knowledge, processes, and skills does our company possess that give us an advantage over our competitors?

Are we better at sales and marketing? Are we better at innovation? Are we better at running a lean operation? Are we better at managing supplier relationships or securing resources? Do we have a better understanding of our customers? Are we better at distributing products? Are we better at squeezing profit out of an operation?

On the other hand, is there stuff we are terrible at? Knowing what we are NOT good at is as important as knowing where we excel.

Look at Microsoft and Apple—clearly two companies that have the resources to be good at many things. But, in reality, each has unique competencies upon which their strategies are built.

ASSUMPTIONS

Knowing what we are NOT good at is as important as knowing where we excel.

The strategic planning paradox: No one knows the future. Yet, we must make plans based on what we think will happen in the future.

We don't know. So, we assume. All strategic plans are therefore built upon assumptions—whether we realize it or not.

Some of those assumptions are based on very measurable, predictable facts such as a growing or shrinking demographic. At other times it's like looking into a room full of bouncing ping pong balls and trying to predict where they are all going to go.

The greatest danger in strategic planning is not "not knowing." The greatest danger is "thinking you know."

The purpose of this section is to quickly put some reality on your assumptions about what will and won't happen in the future. Some assumptions when examined are like mist, not the concrete reality we thought they were.

As you look over your list of issues and insights that you've been building up until now, see which of these categories they fall into. Then ask yourself on a scale of 1–5 how "sure" you are about the reality of each assumption.

1. Things are going to STAY the same.
2. Something is going to STOP happening.
3. Something is going to START happening.
4. Something is going to KEEP happening.
5. Something happening is going to INCREASE in intensity.
6. Something is going to DECREASE in intensity.

The most important factor in this step is realizing that much of what we are basing our hopes and future on is a guess. If we can admit we don't know what is going to happen, we are more prepared to adapt and change if it doesn't come true.

Simply put, you're better off knowing that you don't know—rather than thinking you know what you don't.

N-JOY

Okay, I had to tweak this one a bit to make it fit into the acronym—Author's privilege.

N-joy, enjoy—Passion!

What are you and your team most passionate about?

Logic can only take you so far. It can suggest a direction. It can show dangers. It can highlight an opportunity. But the real drive behind an enterprise is its passion.

Over the years I've discovered that one can do a thorough job of analyzing a business, its customers, and its competitors, and discover an incredible strategic advantage—and it just doesn't matter, because a leader and his team's passion doesn't lean in that direction.

That's both a good and bad thing.

Business journals are full of stories about companies that should have tightened their focus, but the CEO was passionate about a pet acquisition that ultimately led the businesses to ruin.

Yet, what great business victory hasn't been built on the leader's passion?

Strategic thinking often turns up more than one "right" answer. When there is more than one opportunity, perhaps it's time to stop thinking and start following your heart.

So where's your passion? Is it: A passion for growth? A passion for a customer segment? A passion for a vision? A passion for a larger cause or purpose? A passion for a product? A passion for a technology?

Remember, passion is a two-edged sword. Passion is dangerous. It blinds. It biases. It pulls companies away from their strengths and competencies.

And . . .

It changes the world.

What's your passion?

CRITICAL ISSUES

Now it is time to take the big list of frustrations and opportunities, numbers and insights we have collected during our scan, and distill them down to three or four items most likely to have a major impact on our business.

I suggest you whittle this list down to no more than 4 critical issues. In many businesses one critical issue stands above all others in its potential to harm or help the enterprise.

Once you have your narrowed list of critical issues, we are going to bring more light to them through two thinking tools; causes and impacts.

CAUSES

We need to make sure we are focused on the right problems and the right opportunities.

No challenges or opportunities support themselves. They are caused. And, it is important you understand the causes that are driving your problems and opportunities.

Before we jump in and start strategy-making, we need to make sure we are focused on the right problems and the right opportunities.

Often the pain we feel in business is just the symptom of a larger, more serious issue. And the opportunity we see is being caused by a larger force behind it.

So take a look at your major frustrations and opportunities and ask: "What's causing this?"

For example, a company may be feeling the pain of falling sales. They could pounce on that as their major issue and start crafting strategy. Or, they can step back and ask, "Why?" "What's causing our sales to drop?"

After talking with the sales team, they may learn that customers have started buying a competitor's lower-priced product.

But why? Is it just the price? After a little more examination they discover not only is the competitor's product priced lower, but it performs better.

So, it looks like the company's product development has fallen behind the competitors. Again, why?

The business realizes that it has to lower its R&D budget to increase margins, because its operating costs are higher than the competitor's.

So, the root cause is high operations costs relative to the competitors.

That's a dramatically different problem than "falling sales."

Now it's your turn. Take your larger problems and opportunities and put them under the microscope. Ask: "What's causing this? Why?"

IMPLICATIONS

Finally, it's important to have a clear picture of what will happen if a major problem is not dealt with. Or, if a major opportunity is capitalized on.

Think in best- and worse-case scenarios. Then put numbers on it.

If this problem is not dealt with, what's the worst that can happen? What other problems will this cause? What's the ultimate impact of this on our business?

If we pursue this opportunity, what's the best that can happen? What other good things will happen if we successfully pursue this? Ultimately, how much is this going to be worth to our business?

WHERE YOU ARE

Now you know where your business is at. You know what your major frustrations, problems, and challenges are. You know what opportunities are within your grasp. And you know how much impact those critical issues will have on your business.

This insight lets us take the next step: Crafting a compelling vision.

In the following chapter you will use your problems and opportunities as a springboard for creating a compelling vision of what you want your business to become.

3

Vision:
Where Are
You Going?

After being crushed by the unfettered power of tyranny, the U.S. Founding Fathers penned the following Declaration of Independence . . .

> "We hold these truths to be self-evident, that all men are created equal, that they are endowed by their Creator with certain unalienable Rights, that among these are Life, Liberty and the pursuit of Happiness."

Facing the tearing of the Union, 250,000 war dead, and political unrest, President Lincoln declared the following vision:

". . . We here highly resolve that these dead shall not have died in vain, that this nation shall have a new birth of freedom, and that government of the people, by the people, for the people shall not perish from the earth."

Facing an embarrassing, and dangerous, loss to the Soviet Union in the space race, President John Kennedy declared the following vision:

". . . We shall send to the moon 240,000 miles away from the control station in Houston a giant rocket more than 300 feet tall—the length of this football field—made of new metal alloys some of which have not yet been invented, capable of standing heat and stresses several times more than have ever been experienced, fitted together with a precision better than the finest watch, carrying all the equipment needed for propulsion, guidance, control, communications, food, and survival, on an untried mission, to an unknown celestial body and then return it safely to earth re-entering the atmosphere at speeds of over 25,000 miles per hour, causing heat about half that of the temperature of the sun—and do all this and do it right and do it first before this decade is out. . . ."

And facing intense racial hatred, oppression, and bigotry, Martin Luther King had the audacity to declare:

> ". . . I have a dream that one day this nation will rise up and live out the true meaning of its creed: 'We hold these truths to be self-evident, that *all men are created equal'*. . . I have a dream that my four little children will one day live in a nation where they will not be judged by the color of their skin, but by the content of their character . . . All of God's children—black men and white men, Jews and Gentiles, Protestants and Catholics—will be able to join hands and sing in the words of the old Negro spiritual: 'Free at last! Free at last! Thank God Almighty, we are free at last!'"

In this step of the strategic planning process, it is your turn to dream. To hope. To declare a vision of a future that drives you and your team out of today's struggles and challenges into a more profitable tomorrow.

In the previous chapter, you've gotten a realist's view of your business, its challenges, its opportunities, its struggles. But now it's time to do what great leaders throughout history have done: Use those challenges as a springboard to envision a bold future.

Step One, discovering where you are at, was heavy on analysis. Step Two, deciding where you want to go, is heavy on imagination.

Sadly, in most texts on strategy the concept of imagination has been downplayed, or given lip-service, if it is even mentioned at all. Yet, great business achievements owe their birth as much to dreams, vision, and imagination as they do to hard, calculated analysis.

It's easy to understand why imagination is downplayed—strategy shapes the future of the company, you want to face the numbers, be realistic. It is serious business.

Your vision of what your company can become will have more impact on your actions today than where your company has come from.

But the truth is that great strategy is a blend of hard analysis and wild dreaming. The future isn't set in concrete. Your vision and actions determine in large part what happens.

Consider that every day, in cities all over the world, restaurants are started. What explains one that grows into a national or international chain, and the other that remains a local favorite?

Nothing except the vision of the founder. One envisioned a business that served customers well and provided his family a comfortable living. The other envisioned a major regional or national chain. Neither vision is right or wrong. But vision leads the strategy. Strategy is servant to the vision.

Here's a great truth: Your vision of what your company can become will have more impact on your actions today than where your company has come from.

We can't drive a company toward greatness by looking in the rearview mirror, by looking at a balance sheet and imagining just a little more of the same.

So, in this section we are going to imagine more—a lot more. We are going to dream our way past our problems, our balance sheets, and our scarce resources.

Right now, set the book aside and dream.

Consider your challenges and then consider instead what you want to have happen. Don't just think of racism—imagine equality. Don't see a loss—see the moon. Don't dwell on tyranny—dream of freedom.

What is the best possible future you can imagine given your current challenges? How profitable is your company? How many customers do you have? Is your enterprise global, national? What does the press say about your company? What is it like for employees to work at the company? Have you gone public? Have you sold out for hundreds of millions? How is your company serving customers? What greater purpose is the business achieving in the world?

Dream!

After you are finished dreaming your best imaginable future, I want to give you some more elements to dream about. Let's first challenge your notion of "what business you are in."

WHAT BUSINESS ARE YOU IN?

Perhaps you've heard the story of the three bricklayers. A reporter walks up to a new building site in New York City and asks three bricklayers what they are doing.

The first man says, "I'm laying bricks."

"I'm building a wall," says the second.

The third man pauses from his work, glances toward the sky, and says, "I'm building a Cathedral."

"What business are you in?" It's only five words; yet, this is one of the most critical questions you'll ever answer about your business.

"What business are you in?" It's only five words; yet, this is one of the most critical questions you'll ever answer about your business.

Here's why . . .

Your definition of the business is True North. By answering this question in a new way you can revolutionize your opportunities for growth, profits, and competitive advantage.

Your concept of the business governs every other decision you will make about your business. Every single one: the vision you ultimately strive for, whom you perceive to be competitors, whom you choose as customers, what products and services you choose to develop, whom you hire—everything!

If an idea for a new product or service is seen as being outside a business's core identity—then it will be rejected. If an opportunity is perceived to be outside the core identity of the business—it's not pursued.

Yet, as important as the definition of the business is to the future of a business, it is rarely examined or is fuzzy at best.

Typically there are two challenges that businesses face with their core identity.

First, the fact that it's almost subconscious and unquestioned. Therefore, it exerts a hidden influence on key decisions without ever being brought into the light and examined for validity.

The kneejerk identity most businesses default to is, "We are in the widget business." They define themselves by the product or service they create. Ask a lawyer what business she is in and you can expect to hear, "I'm an attorney." And . . . "I'm a labor attorney." Go to the executive suite of an auto manufacturer and you'll get some variation of "We make cars."

Compare these kneejerk responses to how Italian Master Chef Massimo Navarretta responds when asked about what business he is in.

Massimo is the mastermind behind Onotria, an upscale Italian restaurant in Costa Mesa, California. Surprisingly, Massimo doesn't see himself as being in the Italian restaurant business. If you ask him what business he is in, you'll hear, "I'm in the business of creating moments."

When you understand what business Massimo is really in, then you understand why he did away with the typical grass and shrub landscaping in front of the restaurant and planted a small vineyard and herb garden in its place. And you'll understand why many local business people bring their important clients, customers, and contacts to Onotria.

As Massimo says, "We spend our lifetimes to make a contribution in the lives of others. The entity is not important. A grain of sand can make a difference. In your hand a special moment can be the beginning of a lifelong friendship."[2]

If you were opening a restaurant in the same area, who would you rather compete with, a guy in the Italian food business—or a guy in the business of making moments?

In a few paragraphs we'll look at ways you can define your business identity, but, first, let's look at the second challenge many businesses have with their identity: The multiple personalities syndrome.

Since the definition of the business is often subconscious and unexamined, it should be no surprise that key leaders in a company will often have different notions of what business they are actually in. And, it should be no surprise that those identities are closely related to their own departments.

For example, recently I was in a strategy session where the sales VP was adamant that the company was in the business of "increasing clients' sales results" while the VP of technology was vehemently defending the position that they were in the "X Technology" business.

When key members of a

Your decision here will shape the future of the company.

business leadership team have such different perspectives on the core nature of the business, it leads to disjointed decision making, erratic changes in business direction, and disunity between key executives and their departments.

There are many possible answers to what business you are in. And, no single right answer. But answer you must. And your decision here will shape the future of the company.

During the Great Depression, Cadillac faced a crisis. Its sales were plummeting. Competitors were eroding its market share. But then, as Peter Drucker notes in The Essential Drucker, Nicholas Dreystadt redefined the business. No longer would they be selling "transportation." No longer would their competitors be Ford and Chevrolet and Chrysler. Dreystadt's new definition of the business was, "Cadillac competes with diamonds and mink coats. The Cadillac customer does not buy 'transportation' but 'status.'"

This new identity revolutionized Cadillac.

So, how do you go about imagining a new identity for your business?

There are three broad categories that business identities fall into.

1. The product or service produced.
2. The result, benefit, or utility received by the customer.
3. The core competencies of the business.

There is nothing wrong with choosing to define your business by any one of those definitions. The goal is to find a definition that: A) leverages the capabilities of the organization, B) delivers a competitive value proposition to customers, C) gives the business room to grow and prosper.

The number of potential identities you can create for the business is limited only by your imagination.

Let's look at some examples of how you can imagine a different identity for your business in the future.

THE PRODUCT OR SERVICE IDENTITY

By far the most common way for business leaders to define the company is by the product or service they make and deliver.

Let's say I make and sell a CRM software solution to Realtors. What business am I in?

Just some of the possibilities are:

- Real estate software
- Software
- Customer relationship tools
- Technology
- Automated marketing systems

Each of those potential identities will lead the company to a very different future. Each will guide every decision the business leader makes.

And this is important . . .

Each will have its own unique set of competitors. When you ultimately choose the identity for your business, make sure you are up to battling with the competition that definition brings you into contact with.

The major problem with choosing a product definition is that it can focus the business internally on "What we do" and not externally on "What the customer buys."

And that's why Theodore Levitt in his groundbreaking article, "Marketing Myopia," championed a customer-focused business definition.

Let's look at that now.

THE RESULT, OR UTILITY IDENTITY

When choosing a result or utility identity for the business, your vision is squarely focused on what the customer is really buying.

Taking our real estate CRM software example from above, we can expand the possible identity to include being in the business of:

- Increasing sales
- Commission growth
- Referral systems
- Time management solutions
- Business growth
- Competitive advantage

Again, each of these identities allows a business to grow in unique ways, to open up new opportunities for product and service offerings, and to expand or contract the customers who can be targeted.

THE COMPETENCY IDENTITY

The final major category used to define a business by is competency. This looks past what you create or deliver, and gets to the heart of the skills, talents, and core excellence you use to produce your product or service.

Our real estate software business could define their competency as:

- Using software to solve real estate marketing problems
- Using software to solve marketing problems
- Automating time-consuming processes
- Using technology to impact sales
- Coding software
- And many more . . .

Encyclopedia Britannica turned its sales around in the Great Depression when they realized they weren't selling "encyclopedias"—they were selling "knowledge" which created future earning potential for the customer.

Focus is critical to creating both growth and competitive advantage.

Remember, each identity you choose is a box. That's good. It puts boundaries on where you will and will not play the game of business. This brings focus to the company. And focus is critical to creating both growth and competitive advantage.

You just need to make sure the box is not so small that it leaves the business no room to grow or so big that the company's resources are scattered without real direction.

And you need to realize that each box also has its own set of competitors. You need to make sure you have the resources to compete against them. If not, choose another box to play in.

One of the most illustrative examples I've run across of the power of creating a new business identity to alter the fortunes of your business is detailed by Ray Davis in his book Leading for Growth.

When Ray took over as CEO of Umpqua Bank, it had six branches and $140 million in assets.

Davis realized that to grow and compete they would need to change the traditional identity of a bank as being in "banking" or in "financial services." As he studied the situation, he came to realize that they were really in the "retail services" business.

And that identity decision changed everything. They no longer hired tellers with banking experience; they hired tellers from the Gap instead.

They stopped calling their bank locations "branches" and called them "stores" instead.

They altered the training to focus on retail service and sales skills.

They hired retail marketing consultants to remodel the stores into exciting places you would want to actually spend time in.

And they added Internet cafes. They changed their culture, their measurements, and their performance rewards.

The result?

Under Davis' leadership, Umpqua owned the top spot in regional banking market share in just three years. They went from six branches in

Now it is your turn to revolutionize your business . . .

1994 to having 140 stores just 11 years later. And their $140 million in assets catapulted to $7 billion.

Now it is your turn to revolutionize your business . . .

What business are you in?

Is your business laying bricks—or is it building cathedrals?

CORE BUSINESS PURPOSE

Why does your business exist?

Closely related to the first question, "What business are we in?", is a second question to help you think about the future you want to create: "Why do we exist?"

The standard answer in business texts and popular opinion is that a business exists to make a profit, or to increase shareholder value. And it is true that a business must make a profit or cease to exist—period.

But, there are two major problems with having big profits be your only vision . . .

One: Every other business on planet Earth has the same purpose, so there is no goal distinction to separate

"If you look at your business intently enough you will realize that it is a thing managed by you that is giving a service to your fellow men."

you from a million other businesses.

Two: Making a profit doesn't act as a guide to business direction and strategy-making. There are thousands of legitimate ways to make a profit.

Clearly, there is a tension here between idealism and the reality that your business must make a profit.

Writing almost a century ago, Robert Ruxton captured this tension best when he wrote—

> *"If you look at your business intently enough you will realize perhaps what you have never realized before—that it is a thing managed by you that is giving a service to your fellow men."*

And—

> *"As you look and as you ponder, you will begin to aspire to give a better and more perfect service . . . because you will realize that your material success hinges on that . . ."*

"Some men arrive at true service with their eyes fixed
on profit while others arrive at profit with their eyes
fixed on service."

And in this segment, we are going to fix our eyes on the true service your business delivers to humankind.

So, take a look at your customers and at the product and service offerings you deliver to them—and let's focus on the greater service behind them.

Let's take your imagination beyond your current offerings by asking some questions. Why are people really buying your product or service? What need or want or desire does it fulfill? Why is that important in their businesses or lives? How are your customers or employees or communities better off because your business exists?

If your business were actually a nonprofit, what ideals would it pursue without thought of profit?

To help fuel your imagination, use the "Why Technique." For example, a kitchen design and supply business may first begin by answering . . .

"We sell kitchen design equipment and supplies."

Why?

"So that customers can fix up their kitchens."

Why?

"So they can get more storage, more convenience, more style."

Why?

"So they can entertain others better."

Why?

"So they can create richer relationships."

Why?

"So they can have more fulfilling, meaningful lives."

A possible core purpose for this business may be, "A kitchen is the soul of the home. Our company helps you radiate its warmth, embrace others, and create a more fulfilling life."

That's a far different business purpose than "selling kitchen equipment and supplies."

That example gives you an idea of how to take what you do now—and think beyond it to larger purposes your business can serve in the future.

Now it's time to take your dreams and crystallize them into a compelling vision that will serve as the North Star to the rest of your strategic planning. This vision will be specific and have a date on it. It should also be beyond your resources and means to achieve easily.

Look 3–5 years into the future.

Take the most compelling elements from your dream of the future at the beginning of this chapter. Think about what business you are really in. Think about what customer groups or segments you are most passionate about serving —and serve the best. Consider the purpose of your business, what value, product, or service you are really giving customers. And think about your financial goals.

Let's distill those elements down into a vision statement.

By _____ (date 3–5 years in future), we are serving _____ (customer group/segment), by offering them _____ (product, service, ultimate value proposition), and our company is _____ (big financial/market objective).

That's your vision. It will drive the rest of the strategic planning process.

You now know two of the major elements of strategic planning: where you are and where you want to go.

The rest of the planning we will do is figuring out how to get there.

And in the next chapter we confront another great truth of strategic planning. To have a vision is to have obstacles.

The minute you crystallize your vision, obstacles arise to keep you from achieving it. Your strategy must take these very real obstacles into account in order to succeed.

So, let's take a look at the giants standing between where you are now and your vision of the future.

4

Obstacles: What's in Your Way?

The Titanic was thought to be "unsinkable." A single iceberg showed the world otherwise.

And any business leader is wise to consider the lessons of the Titanic when crafting their strategy. Yet, either through pride and hubris or naïveté and ignorance, many fail to consider the possible threats and obstacles to achieving their visions.

Fact: The moment you crystallize your vision, you have obstacles.

Fact: The moment you crystallize your vision, you have obstacles. Competitors, forces, and naysayers align against you. And if your strategy doesn't take them into account, you don't have a strategy.

Being "optimistic" and having a "can-do spirit" are not excuses for failing to examine potential obstacles standing in between you and your objectives.

Imagine a ship's navigator who fails to account for shoals, reefs, islands, and currents in mapping out his passage to their destination. He would endanger the ship and all lives on board.

And what great general doesn't carefully consider his enemies' strengths and his own weaknesses before making a plan for victory?

Planning a great strategy is actually easier when you know the obstacles you face.

Sadly, one of the biggest strategic mistakes business leaders make is failure to take a hard look at the obstacles confronting them.

So I'm not going to let you make that mistake. In this section we are going to first make a list of every possible obstacle you can think of that may block your path to achieving your vision. Then, second, we will narrow that list down to the three obstacles that pose the greatest danger to your success.

This is the shortest section of the strategic planning process, but, going through this step, you'll discover that planning a great strategy is actually easier when you know the obstacles you face.

OBSTACLE IDENTIFICATION

Use this list as a starter to help you identify obstacles in the way of your vision.

- Money
- Time
- Knowledge
- Skills
- People
- Competitors
- Customers
- Offerings: products, services
- Economic forces
- Market forces
- Attitudes and culture
- Doubt and fear

Once you've used this list and your imagination to make a large list of potential obstacles, we move to the second step and isolate the biggest three obstacles we face.

BIGGEST OBSTACLES

Take a look at that list of obstacles. Can any be combined into larger groups? If so combine them.

Now look at it again. What are the three biggest obstacles you face? It's okay if you don't know how to deal with them yet. What is important is to take them into account before we move to crafting your strategy.

Your three biggest obstacles are:

A.
B.
C.

At this point in the strategic planning process you have accomplished a great deal . . .

1. You know where you are. You've identified the problems and opportunities facing you today. You know your most valuable customers. You are aware of your competitors' strengths and weaknesses.

2. You know where you want to go. You've used your frustrations and challenges to imagine a better future for your company. You've thought not just about what's wrong, but you've created a compelling vision of where you want to go.

3. You've now taken a realist's look at what obstacles are standing in between you and where you want to go. This information is critical to consider before ever committing to a strategy.

Now it's time to look at the resources you possess from which you will shape your strategies.

5

Resources:
The Art of
Resourcefulness

Cliff Cooper watched his dream of bringing water to
Texas' Pan-Handle Dust Bowl evaporate in front of
him.

You see, Cliff grew up in the poverty of the Dust
Bowl. Later in life, he was exposed to new vertical well
pump technology and saw its potential in transforming
the land and lives in the Texas High Plains into a fertile
farming region.

Yet, after negotiating contracts with a well-pump
manufacturer, arranging for distribution and financing
throughout the Midwest, setting up service centers, finding well drillers with the right equipment and skill, and
educating dry land farmers about irrigation farming, his

vision (and the crops) were about to be lost over a shortage of simple 6" lap-weld pipe.

The year was 1946 and WWII had created a severe steel shortage. There simply was not enough steel to make the pipe. That meant the farmers would not be able to plant crops, and his dream of transforming the Dust Bowl into fertile farmland was in jeopardy.

One day while driving, Cliff passed an oil field. He realized that all those old dry wells would have miles of pipe. As it turned out, even after the expense of pulling out the pipe and cleaning it, this pipe cost farmers less than the new pipe would have.

As a result of Cliff Cooper's vision, and resourcefulness, the Dust Bowl, and the poverty it created, were eliminated.[3]

The point of this story, and this chapter, is that you have more resources available to help you achieve your vision than you may think.

From your resources, your strategies spring.

At this stage in the strategy process, you've set a vision you don't fully understand how you're going to achieve (if you do, you shot too low), and you're facing obstacles you don't yet know how to overcome.

So it's time to take a good hard look at your resources.

From your resources, your strategies spring.

Over the years, I've discovered that most businesses have far, far more resources than they believe they have. So my goal in this chapter is to help you see more of what you already possess.

VISION MULTIPLES YOUR RESOURCES

First, the mere fact that you have a clear, compelling vision will multiply both the effectiveness of your existing resources—and even define what you consider to be a resource.

A simple illustration will help. Let's say I'm backpacking. It's time to set up camp and I've discovered I didn't pack a hammer to pound in the tent stakes. Before this moment, the rocks scattered around the campsite were just rocks. The minute I have a problem and objective, the rocks suddenly become resources—makeshift hammers.

Now let's say I'm attacked by a bear while cooking up dinner. Suddenly the same rock that was just a rock, then a hammer, is now a survival weapon. The transformation from rock to weapon happened the instant there was a vision and will to survive.

In your business there are a lot of rocks sitting around. As you now re-look at your business through the filter of that vision, you'll discover a lot of those rocks are transformed into valuable resources.

Second, a vision also aligns the resources you know you have so they are all now working together toward the same objective. Imagine Vikings rowing an ancient ship. Many companies with only a fuzzy idea of where they are going, or no idea at all, have the equivalent of some men sitting backward rowing against others rowing forward, with none of their strokes timed. The moment you have a vision, your people, time, competencies and other resources are all rowing in the same direction—together.

ELIMINATE THESE BARRIERS
TO YOUR RESOURCEFULNESS

Third, you'll find your natural resourcefulness multiplied when you eliminate common mental barriers.

FOCUSING ON WHAT
YOU DON'T HAVE

Many leaders discover that when a vision is created, their teams suddenly develop a perverse tendency to generate lists of what resources they don't have to accomplish it. "We don't have the people to put on this . . ." "We don't have enough time for what we are doing now . . ." "We don't have the necessary software . . ." "We've never done this before. We don't have the experience."

During the Vietnam War, the North Vietnamese did not have air superiority. As a result, their bridges along the Ho Chi Minh Trail were often blown out of the water. Instead of focusing on the fact that they didn't possess a better air force, the North Vietnamese focused on their objective: getting supplies across the river. Their rivers are quite muddy. So they came up with the strategy of building their bridges just below the water line. The bridges could no longer be seen from the air. The strategy was so effective that the United States did not learn of its existence until after the war.

> *Focusing on what you don't have is not a path to your vision.*

Focusing on what you don't have is not a path to your vision. It assumes that team members know in advance exactly what strategies and resources they need to succeed. And of course, they don't have them.

FOCUSING ON PROBLEMS AND OBSTACLES

In order for strategic planning to succeed in the real world, you must acknowledge problems and obstacles. But problems and obstacles are not visions. And spending too much time becoming an expert in the problems does nothing to take you toward your vision.

In researching their book Breakthrough Thinking, authors Nadler and Hibino discovered that the most creative executives did not focus on problems much at all. They instead focused on their purposes.

Purpose and vision–focused thinking, rather than problem-focused thinking, is the best way to creatively use your resources. If you are trying to return a system to stasis, for example a broken car or a sick patient, problem-focused and cause-focused thinking are invaluable. But a problem isn't a vision. And often the best way to accomplish your vision is simply to sidestep the problem altogether—not become an expert in it.

MISTAKING STRATEGIES AND TACTICS FOR OBJECTIVES AND VISION

As a business leader, you are probably pretty good at coming up with solutions to problems. With most business leaders, it is instinctive. But, when doing strategic planning, jumping too soon to specific strategic and tactical solutions can fixate your thinking too early in the planning process and blind you to innovative ways to accomplish your vision.

And in many companies, the strategies and tactics become confused with the vision and objectives. Strategies begin to exist for themselves instead of in service to a vision. "We have to do a quarterly client webinar" stops existing as a method of increasing profitability and begins to exist because "we always do a quarterly webinar for clients."

And let's face it, often managers are reluctant to let a strategy go because it is what they do for a living. Their fear is if the strategy is let go—so are they.

ONLY LOOKING INTERNALLY FOR RESOURCES

Another barrier to resourcefulness is limiting the scope of your search for resources to only internal resources.

Your company may not actually have the resources you need internally to reach your vision—but others outside your company may.

Marketing consultant Jay Abraham has shown companies how they can actually use their competitors as resources to increase sales and profits. He points out that after a company has tried to sell their leads X number of times, the likelihood of any of them buying is slim to none. For whatever reason, those prospects have decided not to purchase from the company. So why not sell the leads to competitors who now have a better chance of selling them. Conversely, why not buy from competitors the leads which they couldn't sell?

In fact, businesses within the newsletter industry often sell or rent their prospect list to direct competitors.

Your existing customers may be a great resource of funding, ideas, and manpower. Very often a good customer can be persuaded to pay in advance for products that haven't yet been developed in exchange for a discount or competitive lead time.

For many companies, product development is critical—and often expensive. Yet, there are companies with products that your customers would buy from you. And if your business has a great product, but doesn't have a large existing customer base to sell it to, some companies are more than happy to sell your product to their customers. These joint ventures can give you instant access to markets that have cost others tens of millions of dollars and a decade to create. Those examples may or may not make any sense to your specific strategic situation, but they do show the importance of looking outside the walls of your own company when you are searching for the necessary resources to achieve your vision.

WRONG OBJECTIVES

It is inevitable that during the execution phase of your strategy that something will go wrong somewhere. And when it does, it's easy to try to overcome the problem by spending time and effort on the wrong objectives.

I have a client whose telemarketing tactics were not working as well as they expected. They had begun selling an $1800 training course to the managers of real estate offices. They were selling one out of twenty managers they got phone appointments with—actually very respectable.

But, they wanted to do better.

When we first discussed the tactical challenge, they said their objective was to do a better job handling objections. I asked, "Do you want to do a better job handling objections—or do you want to increase sales?" The obvious answer was, "Increase sales." Focused on this new objec-

By choosing a higher-level objective, their time, knowledge, imaginations, and other resources were multiplied.

tive they were able to devise an entirely new process that boosted closing ratios to 4/20, a 3× increase. By choosing a higher-level objective, their time, knowledge, imaginations, and other resources were multiplied.

The moral of this story is not to accept the first objective you're given. See if there isn't a higher-level objective that your team should be aiming for. If there is, you have just discovered how to dramatically leverage your resources.

THE ULTIMATE RESOURCE

Knowledge is the ultimate resource because it multiplies all other resources.

In the early 70s, The Club of Rome think tank was warning that the world's energy reserves were going to run out. Instead, those reserves rose by more than 50% over the next 20 years. Why? Invention of the fuel injector, knowledge of more effective extraction methods, and lighter, safer cars.[4]

Take advertising. A good advertising manager understands that headlines are a major leverage point when testing a direct response ad, sales letter, or pay-per-click ad. In fact, tests have shown that changing the headline in an ad can increase its effectiveness by 2000%.

By conducting a simple A/B split test, an ad manager who possesses this knowledge can get 300% to 2000% better performance from his resources over his competitor. The only difference is knowledge of testing, and that the headline is a major leverage point.

There are dozens of areas in your business—manufacturing processes, sales processes, segmentation management, manufacturing know-how, finance, accounting, etc.—where knowledge can effectively multiply your resources many times.

But here's the rub . . .

If you knew where those areas were, you would be implementing them right now.

This is why it is so important to seek the support of a wide selection of your team's experience. Different people possess different areas of expertise and specialized knowledge. If your strategic planning process is limited to only a few individuals or only people inside your company, or only a specific function or group, you lose out on the ability to tap into the power of knowledge to multiply your resources.

THE RESOURCE HUNT

Now it is time to reconsider your resources in the light of your vision. Here's a checklist of areas to consider as you look for resources to help you craft your strategy:

- Other people's money, talent, time, resources, knowledge, connections
- Outside experts and perspectives
- Knowledge from books, your people, your stakeholders, experienced advisors
- Competitors' leads, past customers, mistakes, market positions
- Your team's skills and talents
- Customers . . . for knowledge, research, funding, ideas
- Your situation's unique elements
- Major trends whose forces can be harnessed
- Other businesses who serve your customers but do not compete

Beware the
Quadrant of Doom!

Having a bold vision doesn't mean you stop being smart about how you choose to deploy your resources. Yet that is exactly what many companies do when envisioning new markets and products.

In an attempt to avoid competition, to be forward thinking, and to be first to the future, they inadvertently land smack in the quadrant of doom where long sales cycles suck their business under like quicksand.

Let's look at how this works so you can avoid it . . .

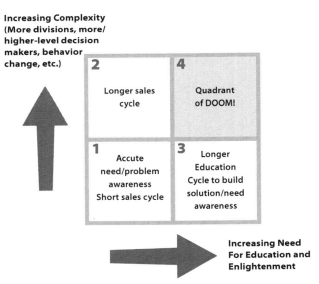

Increasing Complexity (More divisions, more/ higher-level decision makers, behavior change, etc.)

2 Longer sales cycle

4 Quadrant of DOOM!

1 Accute need/problem awareness Short sales cycle

3 Longer Education Cycle to build solution/need awareness

Increasing Need For Education and Enlightenment

In Quadrant 1 you have a customer, usually a single decision maker, who is acutely aware of their problems. They are probably in a lot of pain. And they very often know what products and services can solve their problems. If you are selling in this quadrant, you will have a fast sales cycle. You also may have a lot of competition.

In Quadrant 2 you encounter more complexity and fewer competitors. Here the need is known by the customer, but, the number of decision makers at various management and executive levels increases. The solution may require a complex integration of several technologies, or it may require some behavior change on the part of the organization as well. As you can see in the diagram, as your sales complexity increases, so does your sales cycle.

In Quadrant 3 you have a situation where the customer is not well-informed on the problems or on the products and services you provide to help them. This is often the case with new technology, software, etc. The market may need to be educated to truly understand their problems and their implications. In addition, they need to know what products and services exist to solve them. Again, the more you need to educate a market about problems and solutions, the longer your sales cycle.

Quadrant 4 is the "Quadrant of Doom." Here you are approaching a market that requires complex sales efforts at a high level across many quadrants . . . and . . . this market needs a lot of education about problems and solutions.

Yes, you will likely encounter fewer competitors here. You will also encounter fewer sales.

Over the years I've watched companies get trapped in the Quadrant of Doom, and it is not a pretty death. These businesses struggle to survive for years on sparse sales, dwindling cash flow, and a few fumes of hope that someday the market will reach a turning point and they'll be perfectly positioned to seize it.

It's a deadly game that you should avoid unless you have a core business with very strong sales and cash flow that gives you staying power.

If your vision looks like it is leading you into this quadrant, change the vision. Look for market and product matches that require less complexity and less education.

And if you are currently in the Quadrant of Doom, get out. Find a way to make your solutions require fewer decision makers and target needs that customers realize are causing pain now.

BUT WHAT ABOUT REALITY?

As you go through this process, you may come to the realization that you don't have the resources needed to accomplish your initial vision. Just as in war there are some battles that shouldn't be fought, so in business there are some markets that shouldn't be entered, some competitors it is wise to avoid, and some visions that are beyond your reach. And if your vision is truly out of reach, now is the time to go back and revise the vision before you go through the rest of the strategy-making process.

> *Just as in war there are some battles that shouldn't be fought, so in business there are some markets that shouldn't be entered.*

You will always struggle with the tension between a vision worth striving for and resource constraints.

Many businesses err on the side of creating small visions that don't cause them to rise to new challenges, let alone even tap their unused capacity.

There is an old axiom in sports and business that performance rises to meet expectations. Just as a coach with high expectations can get more performance from his team, you can get more sales, profits, and growth from your business when you raise expectations.

On the other hand, there is such a thing as reality. Some visions are beyond the reach of an enterprise, and to deny that is to set up the business, and your team, for failure.

A few years ago I was in a meeting with a new entrepreneur. He explained to me how his un-launched business, which had no proof-of-concept, would be larger than IBM in just three years. While this gentleman truly believed in his vision, he was destined for failure. And I know of a financing company that decided to grow by purchasing a home DVD gaming company. They had no experience, competence, knowledge, connections, or resources of any kind in that industry. It was an opportunity they should have let pass by.

So how do we manage the tension between a great vision and reality?

Review what you learned during the FAST SCAN phase. If your business fundamentals are strong, you have dominant market share, you have cash reserves, and a strong team, then you can reach for higher objectives in new markets that may require a negative investment and staying power against tough competitors.

However, if you are short on cash, are a small player in a market with tough competitors, and have a new team, then you may consider growing by focusing on a smaller niche market closer to your core competence to begin with.

I know, that sounds like romper-room–level common sense. Yet, take a look at the business press and you'll discover that one of the biggest reasons businesses fail isn't due to physical resources—it's a knowledge gap.

One of the biggest reasons businesses fail isn't due to physical resources—it's a knowledge gap.

Businesses, like bugs to the light, seem to be attracted to products and markets of which they have neither experience nor knowledge. Every year very smart business executives burn through hundreds of millions of shareholders' dollars by letting their visions lure them beyond their experience and competence.

And, every year, small entrepreneurs plant the seeds of great enterprises by focusing on a very small, unexploited segment of a larger market to start.

Very often you can grow your business and profits faster by creating a more focused vision. So, after completing this phase, you may need to reshape your vision to match your resources.

That's not small thinking—it's smart strategy!

Resourcefulness is the ability to see rocks and muddy rivers, competitors and dry oil wells as resources to achieve vision. And, those resources form the raw materials of strategy. So, now that you realize you have more resources than you originally thought, let's look at how to craft your strategy.

6

Strategy:
How Will You
Get There?

D ave Savage, President of SmartReply, faced one of the toughest business decisions of his life . . .

The Federal Trade Commission had just dropped a bomb on his industry limiting how his customers could use his products and services. New competitors were springing up like weeds—then slashing prices by 50% and more just to win any scrap of business that would let them survive.

Worse yet . . .

A new competitor just walked into the industry with a $35 million war chest—and they weren't hesitating to spend it.

Many of Dave's advisors at the time were telling him to diversify into even more industries and niches.

Dave took a hard look at what his ideal client would look like. He sat down and created a list of criteria a "dream" client and industry would meet. They would have:

- A database of 1 million or more customers
- A natural reason to repetitively contact those customers on at least a monthly basis
- A solution for one client could be easily used for another client
- An opportunity to create immediate, bottom-line impact for the client

There was only one segment that met all 4 of those criteria: the retail sector. So, against the counsel of many of his advisors, Dave focused his entire businesses on dominating the retail segment.

This single decision affected how he spent his marketing dollars. Whom he hired for his sales team. Whom he hired to manage clients. Whom he hired to run his marketing. In short—every other decision he made in the business was impacted by his single strategic choice of the ideal customer.

The result?

Dave's counterintuitive decision took his company from being a scrappy, bootstrapped startup, to dominating an industry and generating $7 million a year in revenues just a few short years later. All while his better-funded competitors floundered.

Strategy Matters!

And Dave Savage's story illustrates a few core principles brilliantly:

First, one strategy can often out-produce another strategy by 10 times or more. Same effort, same resources, and 10 times the results. The only difference is where you choose to focus your company resources.

> *One strategy can often out-produce another strategy by 10 times or more.*

Second (and paradoxically), by doing less, you often achieve more.

One of the secrets to strategy's power is focus. Your resources are concentrated where you can do the most good for your customers and yourself.

Simply put, strategy is about saying "No" as much, or more, as it is about saying "Yes."

Third, your strategy should be unique to your vision, obstacles, and resources. There is no one-size-fits-all strategy.

Yes, strategies can be categorized as growth, diversification, focus, offensive, defensive, etc. But in truth, your strategy is often a blend of several of these elements. You're ceasing activities in one aspect of the business while increasing them in another. You're focusing more narrowly to grow.

Grow Your Business
Faster by Doing Less!

I've asked dozens of business owners over the years what their plans are to grow their businesses.

All of them can list a range of strategies they are considering off the top of their heads. Everything from expanding products, going after new markets, starting a new ad campaign, hiring more people, and a hundred other ideas.

Almost always these lists are lists of "more." When a leader hears the word "grow," they think in terms of "do more."

Very rarely do I hear a business leader tell me what he or she is going to "stop" doing in order to grow their business and profits. Yet, reducing their tactics, strategies, customers, and products may be exactly what many businesses need to do in order to grow faster.

Consider this . . .

You have one gallon of water and five plants. In order to keep them all alive, you must spread your scarce resources equally among them.

However, if you want to create a plant that would be the envy of the neighborhood, you would need to make some tough decisions and channel your water to only one or two plants.

This same principle holds true in your business.

Not all products are as profitable, not all customers have as much potential, not all markets are as attractive, and not all tactics are effective.

By making the hard choice to "do less," you can achieve far greater growth and profitability.

Less is often more.

Fourth, being clear on your criteria for success greatly assists you in narrowing your strategies down to the one or two that will have the most impact.

5 STAGES TO CRAFTING A BREAKTHROUGH STRATEGY

Now it is your turn to craft a unique strategy that multiplies your profits. There are 5 stages.

STAGE 1

START MAKING A LIST
OF ALL THE WAYS YOU
CAN ACHIEVE YOUR VISION.

The goal here is to list strategies—the major paths you will take to achieve victory. But the human mind naturally thinks in terms of tactical solutions first. So, we are going to work with the mind and list everything you can possibly think of that will help you achieve your vision.

Look at your vision, look at your obstacles, look at your resources, and start listing as many ideas, strategies, and tactics as you can think of.

STAGE 2

CREATE MAJOR CATEGORIES.

Once your list of ideas is built, we are going to cluster the various tactics into groups and categories. The categories you discover will become your potential strategies.

STAGE 3

NARROW THE LIST BY CRITERIA.

Now you are going to take your list of potential strategies and put them to the test. Most likely, you do not have the resources to pursue four or five strategies all at once. So, we need to focus on which ones will take us the furthest, the fastest with the least effort toward our vision. We screen strategies with a criteria list.

Every situation is unique, so you will need to think through the most important criteria in your situation. To get you started thinking of criteria, here's a list that will apply to most companies:

Time: Which is fastest to implement? How long before you see a payback?

Resources: Money, people, knowledge. Which strategy requires the fewest resources?

Results: Which strategy will create the biggest impact?

Probability: Which strategic path is the safest and most sure?

Now that you have your most important criteria, it's time to move onto the final phase in this stage.

STAGE **4**

SELECT YOUR STRATEGIC FOCUS.

Your goal in this phase is to choose the one to three most effective strategies for your

No matter what strategy you choose, there will be detractors. As a business leader, you simply cannot please everyone.

How To Achieve High-Probability, Low-Risk Growth

The Ansoff Matrix or Growth Matrix below is a proven tool for considering new ways to grow your business. It identifies the four, and only four, ways you can grow.

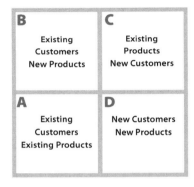

B
Existing
Customers
New Products

C
Existing
Products
New Customers

A
Existing
Customers
Existing Products

D
New Customers
New Products

Quadrant A is a Market Penetration strategy: selling more of your stuff to more of your existing market and customers.

Quadrant B is a Wallet Share strategy: selling new services and products to your existing markets and customers.

Quadrant C is a Market Growth strategy: going after new channels and new markets with your existing product (think baking soda for one of the best examples of this type of growth).

Quadrant D is a Diversification strategy: completely new products and new markets.

But, just as importantly for strategic planning, the Growth Matrix is also a great tool for considering your risk and probabilities of success.

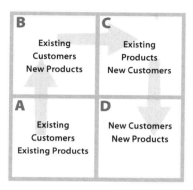

**The lowest-risk,
highest-probability path to take
through the growth matrix**

Usually, the highest-probability, lowest-risk, fastest payback activities you can execute in your business are in Quadrant A. These would include improving the productivity of your existing sales and advertising activities, customer loyalty programs, win-back campaigns to past customers, etc.

Yet, often when planning strategy, business leaders don't focus in this quadrant. They leap to one of the other quadrants first and leave easy profits to their competitors. Experience has shown me that there are breakthrough growth and profit opportunities here for the business leader willing to focus at home before leaping abroad.

Next, before leaping into new markets or channels, consider Quadrant B. Very fast profits can be realized by introducing new products and services to your existing customers.

There are several reasons for this.

It is much harder to create a new customer than to sell something new to a customer who knows and trust you. Some estimates show it takes 5 times more effort and expense to create a new customer.

You already have a relationship with your existing customers. You know their needs. It is easy to do extensive interviews with them so your research is more dependable. And often leading-edge customers will pay to help you develop a new offering for them. So, your new product development can self-fund.

Some argue that by first moving into Quadrant C you are better utilizing your companies existing resources. So, profitability is higher by identifying new markets and segments for your existing offerings. This is true if you don't consider your existing customer relationships as a resource.

When you consider the time, effort, and expense in marketing and selling to someone who has never heard of you, I argue you'll get a much faster, more sure payback by developing new offerings for your existing customers.

Once you have optimized Quadrant A and developed new offerings for your customers in Quadrant B, it is then time to move out into Quadrant C and develop new markets and channels for your existing products and services.

Finally, after you have followed the proven growth path through the matrix, you can consider Quadrant D: Diversification.

Unfortunately, many businesses leap into Quadrant D first when considering growth. Big mistake. Here's why. . . .

In Quadrant D you have no competency, no track record, no knowledge. Simply put, you have no clue. That means a brutal learning curve while battling better armed-competitors. If you are lucky, Quadrant D can be a Blue Ocean. But just as often, it is a Black Hole that pulls your business toward its destruction.

There are only two types of businesses that should consider a leap into this quadrant. First is a business that is successfully exploiting all the other quadrants. In this case you have a business that has the resources needed to survive the learning curve you will face in Quadrant D. Here, the penalty for failure is not fatal to the business. And you gain the safety of diversification when successful.

Second is the business that has no choice. Either brutal competition or government regulation have wiped out their existing business model. So, the only strategy left to them is a running leap into Quadrant D.

In summary, you can achieve fast, profitable, and secure growth by following this proven path through the growth matrix. Seize the easy profits in markets you know before venturing into less sure (yet, admittedly more attractive) possibilities farther from home.

unique situation. And we are going to use the criteria you chose in the previous stage as a screen.

Simply make a grid with the criteria on one axis and the strategies on the other. Now choose the strategies that best meet the criteria.

THE X FACTOR

Often when business leaders take their teams through an exercise like this, the winning strategy is not the strategy the team wanted to win. When this happens, you need to take a hard look at two considerations.

1. Your team's intuition is wrong. The winning strategy should have won. That's the reason we create logical criteria.
2. Your team's intuition is right, and the analysis is wrong. There are factors that a criteria list may

not pick up, but that are nonetheless important, and the team's intuition is picking up on it.

What to do? Give serious consideration to following the strategic choice that has the most passion around it. Even if it isn't the "most right" choice—it may be the choice that gets the most energy, enthusiasm, and support behind it.

STAGE 5

DECIDE HOW YOU
WILL MEASURE SUCCESS.

How will you know if your strategy is working or not?

In this stage you are going to choose specific qualitative and quantitative measures that define the success of your chosen strategies. Each strategy should have its own measurements. The more specific the measures you choose, the more clarity you and your team will have about whether you're winning or losing.

Qualitative measures such as satisfaction, goodwill, and employee morale have their place. But you should also choose quantitative measures such as units sold, market share, ROI, and other Key Performance Indicators.

YOU CAN'T PLEASE EVERYONE

No matter what strategy you choose, there will be detractors. As a business leader, you simply cannot please everyone. You have to make hard choices and stick with them.

Allowing the organization to pursue too many strategies will dissipate its resources and leave it in danger.

Consider the wisdom of this fable as you choose your strategy . . .

An old man, a boy, and a donkey were going into town. The boy rode on the donkey and the old man walked. As they went along, they passed some people who remarked it was a shame the old man was walking and the boy was riding.

The man and the boy thought maybe the critics were right, so they changed positions.

Later, they passed some people who remarked, "What a shame, he makes that little boy walk."

So, they decided they'd both walk. Soon, they passed some more folks who thought they were stupid to walk when they had a good donkey to ride. So, they both rode the donkey.

Now they passed some people who shamed them by saying how awful to put such a load on a poor donkey.

The boy and the man figured they were probably right, so they decided to carry the donkey. As they crossed a bridge, they slipped, lost their grip, and the donkey fell into the river and drowned.

Moral of the story?

If you try to please everyone, you might as well . . . kiss your ass goodbye.

As a business leader, you've done your best in examining your resources, crafting a vision, and taking a hard look at obstacles. Now you must make an important choice. And saying "yes" to this choice means you are saying "no" to choices that other folks have a stake in. This isn't comfortable, but allowing the organization to pursue too many strategies will dissipate its resources and leave it in danger.

Now that you have made your strategic choice, it's time to focus on the tactics that will power your strategy and carry your vision through.

Tactics:
Who's Doing
What by When?

7

For want of a nail the shoe was lost.

For want of a shoe the horse was lost.

For want of a horse the rider was lost.

For want of a rider the battle was lost.

For want of a battle the kingdom was lost.

And all for the want of a horseshoe nail.

Fact: Your strategies, your vision, and your future rest on great execution of your tactics. Time and again I've seen small tactical shifts create strategic level breakthroughs. And just as often I've seen failures at the tactical level cripple strategic results.

Take the space shuttle Challenger for example. Next to the purposes of the craft and overall design, the O-ring was a relatively small detail—until it failed. Strategies (and businesses) fail because of poor tactical execution.

Anytime you undertake new strategies, there is a good chance that you will need to execute new tactics. "New" means not done before, and that carries some important implications for your choice and execution of tactics.

TACTICS REQUIRE COMMITMENT

First, many times when a company tries out new a new tactic they are nervous about that tactic's prospects for success. This nervousness creates bet-hedging. Being cautious with new tactics is prudent. I'm a proponent of testing before full financial commitment, but under-funding, under-committing, and under-resourcing a tactic does nothing but set it up for failure.

Sometimes just 10% more commitment would create a successful new initiative—but for lack of that 10% the entire 100% is lost.

For a jet to take off from the runway, it needs to have a minimum number of engines and thrust and wing lift. If you take away an engine or two, the plane can't take off. If you try to take off, you will crash.

As silly as that example is, I see its equivalent every day in businesses. They try to launch new tactics but don't give them adequate funding, time, or expertise. As a result, the tactic crashes. Sometimes just 10% more commitment would create a successful new initiative—but for lack of that 10% the entire 100% is lost.

TACTICS REQUIRE LEARNING

Related to this is a failure to understand that new tactics require a business to go through a learning curve. Often the first few attempts at a tactic do not work. That's a fact of life. Yet, as business leaders, we often let our impatience for success cause us to abandon tactics before they have had a chance to move through the learning curve.

Organizations are made up of people. And Abraham Maslow identified the fact that people have a universal learning process . . .

Unconscious incompetence: They aren't aware they are incompetent. And, in our case, they may not even be aware that a given tactic exists to help them achieve the strategy.

Incompetence: They now are consciously aware that a tactic exists—and that they are not very good at it.

Conscious competence: They can successfully implement a tactic—but it takes a lot of conscious effort.

Unconscious competence: The ability and tactics become second nature to the individual and the business.

You have to give your team members enough time and training to master the execution of the new tactics.

TACTICS REQUIRE
THE RIGHT PEOPLE

Getting tactics executed relies on people. Things go a lot smoother if you choose the right people to execute the tactics.

A team member who excels at executing an existing tactic may not be the right team member to execute the new tactic.

A team member who excels at executing an existing tactic may not be the right team member to execute the new tactic.

As we learned earlier tactics require time, skill, and learning to execute successfully. Finding people who have already mastered those elements is often the better choice than trying to force-fit people into new jobs and accountabilities for which they have no skill, no competence, and no passion.

A company I worked with a few years ago decided to add direct mail to its marketing tactics. Naturally, their existing marketing manager took on the task. Working with a designer, he created a beautiful full-color brochure promoting one of their events. They mailed it to 20,000 people. They made one sale.

The company decided that direct mail didn't work for their market. A year later they had a new marketing manager. He suggested the business try direct mail. "Direct mail doesn't work in our industry, we've tried it," he was told. But this manager had unique expertise in direct mail and begged for a chance to prove it could work. They told him he could only mail to 6,000 people. So, he wrote a simple four-page letter. No color. No fancy graphics or artwork. Within one week, $395,000 in orders came in.

What was the difference in the two? Unique knowledge and expertise of the specific tactic.

Your business can save tens of thousands of dollars and years of trial and error by simply putting the right person at the helm of the tactic.

And, if you can't hire the expertise, rent it by bringing in tactical experts to advise your team members.

TACTICS REQUIRE ACCOUNTABILITY

Much tactical failure in companies can be traced to a simple lack of accountability. The old maxim "You don't get what you expect, you get what you inspect" is very true. You must create a regular accountability schedule in place to ensure your team members are moving the tactics and initiatives forward on time and on budget.

THE PROCESS

The process we'll use for creating your tactics will be the same as for creating your strategies. For each strategy you'll list all the possible tactics you can think of. Then we'll filter them through a criteria screen to make sure time is spent only on the most viable, high-impact tactics. Then we are going to assign deadlines and responsibilities to them.

Let's start . . .

STAGE 1
IDEATION

Take your first strategy and start asking, "How might we accomplish this strategy?"

Generate as many ideas and possibilities as possible. Then generate some more. You already have a head start on this process from the previous stage when you combined and clustered your tactics into the larger strategies you wanted to accomplish. Add those ideas to this list.

At this point, if you haven't brought in outside experts to help you with your strategy making, I strongly encourage you to do it now.

None of us know what we don't know. Often someone from a different industry, department, or area of expertise can take a look at the strategy we are tying to achieve and think of simple, effective, powerful ways to accomplish it that never would have occurred to us.

STAGE **2**

SELECTION

Allow me to repeat it again: Strategy is focus. We can't do everything. So, now we need to look at our list of tactical ideas and choose only those that will make the biggest impact on our strategy the fastest, and we do this by passing them through a criteria screen.

> *Strategy is focus. We can't do everything.*

At a minimum your criteria will be Money, Time, Effort, and Competence. You will also generate criteria that are unique to your strategic challenge.

STAGE **3**

RESPONSIBILITY AND DEADLINES

The tactics you've chosen now need to be assigned to specific individuals who will be responsible for execution. Tactics also need a deadline put on them. So, for each tactic, note when it is to be done and who is responsible. Depending on the complexity of your particular tactics, you may want to use project planning software.

If your personal leadership style is stronger with vision and broad strategy, then this stage of the process will be one of the toughest for you. I encourage you to bring in a detail-oriented, tactical planner to your strategic team to help you get your vision down to the critical tactical actions that must occur for you to succeed.

Of course, if you are strong at details and execution, you're thinking that this was the first usable chapter in the book! May I suggest you bring on someone who is a little better at dreaming and scheming to help you with the earlier steps in this process?

You and your team have put in a lot of work to get to this step in the process. And you deserve to feel a sense of accomplishment at completing a strategic planning process all the way from a good situation analysis through vision creation down to the concrete, practical action stages of tactics.

But, there is one more important element for you to succeed in achieving your vision. Let's look at it now. . . .

8

Monitor:
How Are
We Doing?

Las Vegas is known for gambling, but one of the most interesting bets took place at 30,000 feet above the desert just outside the city.

Here, the best fighter pilots in the world came to take a bet made by a cocky, irascible, cigar-smoking, fighter–instructor named John Boyd.

Boyd was an instructor at the Fighter Weapons School and had a standing bet: Put him in a position of disadvantage in front of you like a sitting duck, and within only 40 seconds he would be in a position to shoot you down or he'd pay you $40 and buy you a steak dinner.

Despite the finest fighter jocks in the world taking the bet, Boyd never lost. This earned him the nickname "40-second Boyd."

John Boyd went on to revolutionize how air combat is taught in every air force in the world, was the Godfather behind the F-15 and F-16 fighters, and then changed the way America fights wars with his theories on maneuver warfare adopted by the Marine Corps.

But what's most important to you and your business is his major theory behind these victories: The OODA Loop or Boyd Cycle.

You see, Boyd was bothered by an anomaly he observed studying fighter kill ratios from the Korean War. By all standards, the Soviet MIG-15 was a superior fighter to the U.S. F-86 Saber. Yet, the Saber enjoyed a kill ratio of 10:1 during the Korean War.

Why?

Boyd came to understand that the F-86 had two advantages. It had a cockpit which gave better visibility to the pilot. And the controls were hydraulic—so the plane responded faster and with less effort to the pilot's commands.

Those two facts gave Boyd the insight that the battle went to the fighter who could Observe, Orient, Decide, and Act faster than the other.

His insight not only revolutionized how modern warfare is conducted by the U.S., but it can also revolutionize your business.

You see, there are two major strategic planning errors companies make: 1) They don't do formal strategic planning. 2) They believe once a strategic plan has been created that their success is guaranteed.

In your case, you've been working through your strategic planning with the help of this book. So, you've avoided mistake number one. But I see too many companies go through a formal planning process (the observation, orienting, deciding, and acting); then forget that planning is a loop—that they then have to observe again what is happening in the real world as they implement their strategies.

There are several possible causes for this failure. . . .

First, arrogance. Many consider a strategic plan they have crafted as written by the finger of God in stone—that success is guaranteed.

Second, failure to appreciate how dynamic today's business environment is. Record manufacturers were not doomed by their fellow record manufacturers; they were taken out by a new technology—CDs. In the same way, companies making CDs were not hurt by their fellow CD manufacturers—they got blind-sided by the digital music revolution.

Further, competitors generally don't just sit there when your strategy starts to hurt them. They start reacting. And today's technologies allow them to react faster than ever.

Third, no matter how thorough your analysis, no one has perfect knowledge. To steal a line from the Apostle Paul, "We see through a glass darkly."

Fourth, just because we think a strategy is great doesn't mean our customers will think it is great. Even with the rigorous research you have done, consumers may not embrace the products, services, messages, or channels you approach them with.

Those four facts necessitate your constant vigilance to ensure your strategy is in fact working.

And you can't know if it is working or not without clear measures, milestones, and monitoring. This is the reason we had you put a hard, tangible number on your strategies in a previous step. Those numbers will be your early warning system, alerting you when your strategy is off course.

When you notice that you are not getting the results you want, there are four levels in which to consider making adjustments.

MONITOR EXECUTION

1 The execution level: Is your team actually implementing the strategy and its tactics?

If your team is not executing at the tactical level, consider these two common reasons for tactical failure: Poor execution and misaligned rewards.

It may be simply a lack of performance on the team members' part.

Perhaps they need more accountability and management. Maybe they don't have the skills the new strategy and tactics demand of them.

As I write this, I know of a company who decided one of their tactics was going to be pay-per-click advertising. They began spending $6,000 a month through a nationally respected pay-per-click management company. The results were terrible.

Then one of the employees noticed that their ads weren't showing up near the top of search rankings. They brought in a consultant who discovered gross mismanagement on the part of the pay-per-click company. Instead of dropping the tactic of pay-per-click, they simply switched management firms, resulting in a 75% increase in leads.

You've no doubt heard a business owner say that direct mail doesn't work, email marketing doesn't work, social media doesn't work, blogs don't work, Six Sigma doesn't work, etc. The fact is other companies are using these same tactics and achieving success. Often the problem is just plain bad execution.

Second, make sure the rewards and penalties are aligned with the results you want.

I worked with a business owner who was very frustrated the sales people were not focusing on the products he wanted them to sell. A look at the commission structures told the story. It was simply far more profitable for sales people to move in a direction opposite to what the business owner wanted. This doesn't occur only in sales—it impacts managers and executives all the way to the CEO.

So, before you throw out tactics, first consider whether or not they are being executed correctly.

MONITOR TACTICS

2 The tactical level: It's a fact of life that sometimes our chosen tactics are just not going to work. And, at other times, one tactic will outperform another by 100%.

Tactics aren't strategies. Often companies confuse the two. And when a tactic isn't working, they abandon the strategy instead of testing out a different tactic.

Take for example product development as a strategy. Time and again companies bet all their resources on a single product innovation. When that doesn't achieve the market acceptance they hoped for, they abandon the product development strategy altogether.

Yet, often the problem isn't their strategy, it's the specific tactics they chose to implement the strategy. Had they spread their resources over two or three innovations, sought customer feedback during the development process, and then thrown their major resources behind the winner, they may have had a spectacular win.

Before you abandon your strategy, first consider if the problem is the chosen tactics. Ask: "How else can we achieve this strategy?"

MONITOR STRATEGIES

3 The strategic level: Just as tactics may fail for poor implementation and strategies may fail for wrong tactics, so visions may not be reached because of the wrong choice of strategies.

Before you abandon your strategy, first consider if the problem is the chosen tactics. Ask: "How else can we achieve this strategy?"

In the Preface of this book you read about the "48 million dollar difference." Two companies in the same industry: One struggles, the other sells for $48 million. This is a true story about two entrepreneurs in the mortgage industry. One chose the strategy of focusing on the purchase market. The other chose the refinance market as its main focus. That strategic choice sealed both their fates. The purchase shop continued to struggle given the market conditions of the time. The refinance shop experienced skyrocket growth.

Before you abandon your vision of the future, first consider the major strategic choices you have made. It may be time to switch strategies.

MONITOR YOUR VISION

4 Vision level: Occasionally, despite our best judgment, we come to a realization that we have chosen the wrong vision to pursue. This is one of the most difficult and painful decisions to be made by a business leader.

None of us are gifted with knowledge of what tomorrow will bring. Despite our best efforts, "stuff" happens. Industries are disrupted by unseen innovations. Team members betray. Governments change the rules of the game. Growing economies crash suddenly.

Abandoning an important vision is painful. All of us are born with a will to win. We are taught from childhood not to quit. For this reason, many business leaders are too late when they make the decision to change their vision and alter the direction of their enterprises.

THE LEADER'S PARADOX

As a business leader, you face a great tension: Never quit vs. survive to fight another day.

You may have heard the tale about the man who purchased a gold mine. He mined until he was broke, and then sold the mine to a second man. This man dug three more feet and discovered gold and great riches. The instinct most business leaders have is to find a way to just dig one more foot . . . and then another . . . until success is theirs.

There is truth in that. Persistence and downright stubborn tenacity in pursuit of a vision are responsible for many successes.

But there is another truth. Sometimes stubbornness gets everyone killed. And the first rule when finding yourself in a hole is to stop digging. The mighty oak often snaps in a great wind, while the flexible palm yields enough not to be destroyed.

Before giving up on your vision, first consider if your challenges are born of the wrong strategy, the wrong tactics, or poor execution. But if your problem is that your vision is the wrong fit for your company, then it is better to flex and choose another destination, rather than watch your business snapped apart.

It is better to flex and choose another course, rather than watch your business snapped apart.

And remember the lessons of the fighter pilot 40-second Boyd. Constantly work through your cycles of Observation, Orientation, Decision, and Action. Don't forget these are a loop. You don't do them just once. You act: Then observe the results those actions are creating and make new decisions.

And if you go through this cycle more rapidly than your competitors, you are more likely to emerge victorious.

Notes

1. Tzu, Sun (1990) *The Art of War—Sun Tzu* (edited by James Clavell). Hodder & Stoughton. p. 13.

2. Personal interview with Massimo Navarretta, 2009.

3. Cooper, C. D. (1992) *The Runt Pig Principle: A Fundamental Approach to Solving Problems and Creating Value.* Alliance for Progress Publishers. pp. 103–105.

4. Pilzer, P. Z. (2007) *God Wants You To Be Rich: How and Why Everyone Can Enjoy Material and Spiritual Wealth in Our Abundant World.* Touchstone Faith. pp. 51–52.

Bibliography

Andersen, E. (2009) *Being Strategic: Plan for Success; Outthink Your Competitors; Stay Ahead of Cha.* St. Martin's Press.

Barksdale, S., & Lund, T. (2006) *10 Steps to Successful Strategic Planning.* ASTD Press.

Basadur, M. (1995) *The Power of Innovation: How to Make Innovation a Way of Life & How to Put Creative Solutions to Work.* Financial Times/Prentice Hall.

Birnbaum, W. S. (1990) *If Your Strategy Is So Terrific, How Come It Doesn't Work?* AMACOM/American Management Association.

Bossidy, L., & Ram, C. (2004) Confronting Reality: Doing What Matters To Get Things Right. Crown Business.

Boyd, J. R. (1987) *A Discourse on Winning and Losing.* Maxwell Air Force Base, AL: Air University Library Document No. M-U 43947 (Briefing slides).

Bradford, R. W. (2000) *Simplified Strategic Planning: The No-Nonsense Guide for Busy People Who Want Results Fast.* Chandler House Press.

Charan, R., & Tichy, N. (2000) *Every Business Is a Growth Business: How Your Company Can Prosper Year After Year.* Crown Business.

Collins, J. C. (2002) *Good to Great, Why Some Companies Make the Leap.and Other's Don't.* Harperbusiness.

Cooper, C. D. (1992) *The Runt Pig Principle: A Fundamental Approach to Solving Problems and Creating Value.* Alliance for Progress Publishers.

Davis, R. P., & Shrader, A. (2007) *Leading for Growth: How Umpqua Bank Got Cool and Created a Culture of Greatness.* Jossey-Bass/Wiley.

Drucker, P. F. (2008) *The Essential Drucker: The Best of Sixty Years of Peter Drucker's Essential Writings on Management* (Collins Business Essentials). Harper Paperbacks.

Dudik, E. M. (2000) *Strategic Renaissace: New Thinking and Innovative Tools To Create Great Corporate Strategies.* Using Insights from History and Science. AMACOM.

Fritz, R. (1989) Path of Least Resistance: Learning To Become the Creative Force in Your Own Life. Ballantine Books.

Hamel, G., & Prahalad, C. K. (1969) *Competing for the Future*. Harvard Business School Press.

Johnson, J. E., & Smith, A. M. (2006) 60 Minute Strategic Plan. 60 Minute Strategic Plan Inc.

Kim, W. C., & Mauborgne, R. (2005) *Blue Ocean Strategy: How to Create Uncontested Market Space and Make Competition Irrelevant*. Harvard Business Press.

Koch, R. (1998) The 80/20 Principle—The Secret of Achieving More With Less. Nicholas Brealey Publishing

Markides, C., & Markides, C. C. (1999) *All the Right Moves: A Guide to Crafting Breakthrough Strategy*. Harvard Business Press.

Mrazek, J. E. (1968) The Art of Winning Wars. Walker.

Nadler, G., & Shozo, H. (1990) *Breakthrough Thinking*. Prima.

Pate, C., & Platt, H. (2002) *The Phoenix Effect: 9 Revitalizing Strategies No Business Can Do Without*. Wiley.

Pilzer, P. Z. (2007) *God Wants You to Be Rich: How and Why Everyone Can Enjoy Material and Spiritual Wealth in Our Abundant World*. Touchstone Faith.

Porter, M. E. (1998*) On Competition*. Harvard Business School Press.

Ries, A. (2005) *Focus: The Future of Your Company Depends on It*. Harper Paperbacks.

Robert, M. (1997) *Strategy Pure & Simple II: How Winning Companies Dominate Their Competitors*. McGraw-Hill.

Schaffer, R. H. (1988) The breakthrough strategy: Using short-term successes to build the high performance organization. Ballinger Pub. Co.

Schnaars, S. P. (1997) Marketing Strategy, Customers & Competition (2nd edition). Free Press.

Sun Tzu (1990) *The Art of War—Sun Tzu* (edited by James Clavell). Hodder & Stoughton.

U. S. Marine Corps (1989) *WARFIGHTING, FMFM 1.* U. S. Government Printing Office.

Acknowledgements

First I want to thank my parents who supported and encouraged their son who had serial entrepreneurial instincts. I can only imagine their frustration as their son came home each week with the Next Big Idea. The two of you are the perfect blend of imagination, insight, and wisdom. Thanks for your guidance, understanding, support, and encouragement over the years. And dad, thanks for the name of my business and title of this book.

I also want to acknowledge the group of daring dreamers and doers: the entrepreneurial leaders I had the opportunity to work with over the last 20 years. My clients, often my friends, always my teachers.

Among these leaders, a few stand out for special thanks for taking a chance on me during the early days:

Dave Savage, John Kirker, Mike, Matt, and Tom Ferry, Jay Abraham, Todd Duncan, Don Hobbs.

Bill Mitchell, who pointed out that base hits are just as important as always "swinging from the heels" and "waiting for the perfect pitch."

Strange as it may seem, one of the important ideas behind this book was given flight 34 years ago in the unlikely place of a county swimming pool in Elk Grove, California. My growth spurt was later in life, so I found myself struggling to tag the larger, faster boys in a game of swim pool tag. One of the lifeguards called me over to the guard tower. He looked down at me and said: "Robert, stop trying to out-swim them—start out-thinking them."

There isn't a month that goes by without those words echoing through time as I work with clients who are facing tough competitors. So 34 years later I am now able to thank that lifeguard: Curtis J. Edwards, MD, FACS, General Surgeon and Flight Surgeon.

And I can't forget to say thanks to Terry Osterhout and the gang at The Lost Bean coffee house in Tustin. They graciously tolerated me camping out in their best window seat during the months I worked on this manuscript.

Finally, this book is far more readable thanks to the efforts of my editor, Kathleen Erickson. She suffered so you didn't have to. And thank you Michael Rohani for wonderful work on the design.

Index

A

abandon, 89, 100, 101
ability, 2, 9, 67, 72, 89
Abraham, Jay, 63, 89, 112
accountability, 91, 99
achievements, 15, 36
action, 94
activities, 75, 81
adapt, 6, 8, 28
adjustments, 8, 98
advantage, 22, 26, 29, 38, 44, 45
adversaries, 16, 19
advertising, 66, 81, 99
advisors, 67, 73, 74
Alliance, 105, 108
analysis, 12, 24, 35, 36, 83, 94, 97
Ansoff Matrix, 80
Apostle Paul, 97
Apple, 26
approach, 17, 98
arrogance, 97
Art of War, 11
assets, 46, 47
assumptions, 27
Attitudes, 55

B

backpacking, 59
barriers, 60
bear, 6, 59
behavior, 68, 69
believe, 14, 59, 97
billionaires, 4
birth, 34, 36
blend, 14, 36, 75, 111
blind, 62, 97
blogs, 99
bootstrapped, 74
Bowl, 57, 58
Boyd, John, 95, 96
breakthrough, 81
bricklayers, 38
bridge, 86
brochure, 90
budget, 31, 91

C

Cadillac, 41, 42
cafes, 46
California, 39
campaign, 76
campsite, 6, 59
capabilities, 42
capacity, 70

capital, 25
CD, 19, 97
CEO, 29, 46, 100
Challenger, 87
challenges, 5, 9, 15, 26, 30, 32, 35, 37, 39, 56, 70
channels, 16, 80, 81, 82, 98
checklist, 67
Chevrolet, 41
Chinese, 1
Chrysler, 41
clarity, 24, 84
Club of Rome, 65
Cole, Dandridge, 9
competencies, 12, 26, 29, 42, 60
competency, 44, 45, 82
competition, 17, 18, 43, 68, 83
competitive, 16, 22, 23, 38, 42, 45, 64, 74
competitors, 3, 12, 16, 19, 20, 23, 26, 29, 31, 38, 41, 43, 46, 56, 63, 69, 70, 71, 72, 73, 75, 81, 82, 97, 104
complaints, 25
complexity, 3, 69, 93
concentration, 4
considerations, 83
constraints, 70
consumers, 20, 21, 98
convenience, 49
Cooper, Cliff, 57, 58
core competencies, 26
costs, 16, 31
counsel, 74
counterintuitive, 74
criteria, 74, 77, 79, 83, 92, 93
critics, 85

CRM, 43, 44
culture, 46, 55
cycles, 68, 103

D
Davis, Ray, 46, 47
deadlines, 92
decision, 12, 38, 41, 43, 46, 68, 69, 74, 102
decisions, 17, 19, 39, 73, 76, 102, 103
Declaration of Independence, 33
definition of business, 38, 39, 40, 41, 42, 43
demographics, 22, 24
Depression, 41, 45
deregulation, 23
design, 49, 87, 112
details, 7, 94
detractors, 79, 85
direction, 7, 12, 23, 24, 28, 29, 41, 45, 48, 60, 99, 102
discount, 64
dissipate, 85, 86
distinction, 47
distribution, 57
diversification, 75, 82
diversify, 73
dream, 35, 37, 50, 57, 58, 74
Dreystadt, Nicholas, 41
Drucker, 41, 108
DVD, 71

E
EBITA, 25
effectiveness, 59, 66
efficiency, 22
effort, 64, 75, 79, 81, 82, 89, 96
employees, 20, 37, 49, 99

Encyclopedia Britannica, 45
enemies, 54
enjoy, 28
entrepreneurs, 72, 101
environment, 12, 97
envision, 35
excellence, 44
execution, 64, 87, 88, 89, 93, 94, 98, 99, 103
expense, 58, 81, 82
experience, 46, 60, 66, 71, 72
expertise, 66, 88, 91, 92
experts, 44, 67, 91, 92

F

factors, 20, 21, 83
failure, 54, 71, 82, 88, 89, 91, 97, 98
FAST SCAN, 13, 14, 71
Federal Trade Commission, 73
feedback, 100
firefighting, 24
fixate, 13, 62
focus, 29, 43, 45, 46, 49, 62, 75, 79, 81, 86, 93, 101
forces, 53, 55, 67
Ford, 41
frequency, 21
frustrations, 9, 14, 15, 30, 31, 32, 56
fundamentals, 71
funding, 24, 63, 67, 88
fuzzy, 39, 60

G

Gap, 46
Geographics, 21
giants, 51
global, 21, 37

goal, 14, 42, 47, 59, 78, 79
goals, 2, 50
God, 35, 97, 105, 109
goodwill, 84
government, 23, 34, 83
guide, 43, 48

H

hammer, 6, 59
headlines, 66
hedging, 88
Helmuth Carl Bernard von Moltke, 8
Hibino, 61
Ho Chi Minh Trail, 61
household, 20
Houston, 34
hubris, 53

I

IBM, 71
iceberg, 53
ideals, 49
identity, 39, 40, 42, 43, 44, 45, 46
ignorance, 53
imagination, 4, 6, 7, 35, 36, 42, 49, 55, 111
impatience, 89
implement, 79, 89, 97, 100
implications, 16, 69, 88
incompetence, 89
Indicators, 84
industry, 20, 63, 71, 73, 74, 91, 92, 101
influence, 24, 39
initiatives, 91
innovation, 15, 19, 26, 100
insights, 27, 30

integration, 69
international, 36
Internet, 24, 46
intuition, 83, 84
investment, 71
issues, 2, 14, 15, 27, 30, 32
K
Kennedy, John, 34
knowledge, 26, 45, 65, 66, 67,
71, 72, 79, 82, 91, 97
L
Las Vegas, 95
leadership, 41, 47, 93
leadingedge, 82
leverage, 65, 66
Levitt, Theodore, 43
lifestyle, 21
M
magic, 2, 4
manage, 71, 74
Management, 107, 108
manager, 66, 90, 91
maneuver warfare, 96
manufacturers, 19, 22, 97
margins, 31
Marine Corps, 96
Mark Twain, 11
marketing, 26, 43, 45, 46, 74,
82, 90, 99
Marketing Myopia, 43
Martin Luther King, 35, 107
Maslow, Abraham, 89
materials, 72
measurements, 24, 46, 84
measures, 26, 84, 98
mediums, 16
Microsoft, 26

MIG, 96
misaligned, 98
mismanagement, 99
mission, 34
Monitor, 95, 97, 99, 101, 103
morale, 15, 84
muddy river, 61, 72
N
Nadler, 61, 109
national, 36, 37
Navarretta, Massimo, 39, 105
navigator, 54
naysayers, 53
na√Øvet√©, 53
needs, 6, 69, 82, 88
negative, 71
negativity, 15
negotiating, 57
New York City, 38
niche, 71
North Vietnamese, 60, 61
numbers, 24, 25, 30, 32, 36, 98
O
objections, 65
objectives, 2, 54, 62, 64, 71
obstacles, 5, 6, 7, 51, 53, 54, 55,
56, 58, 61, 75, 78, 86
offerings, 19, 44, 49, 82
Onotria, 39, 40
OODA Loop, 96
operations, 31
opinion, 24, 47
optimists, 15
outperform, 100
P
paradox, 27
paranoia, 3

passion, 28, 29, 84, 90, 113
path, 7, 24, 54, 61, 79, 81, 82,
    83
penalties, 99
performance, 46, 66, 70, 98,
    110
perspectives, 41, 67
pessimist, 6
pilot, 96, 103
position, 20, 41, 95
possibilities, 43, 83, 92
potential, 12, 30, 42, 43, 45,
    54, 55, 57, 77, 78
pp, 105
practical, 94
predict, 9, 27
prevention, 22
price, 31, 74
probability, 81
processes, 26, 45, 66
profitability, 16, 62, 77, 82
proposition, 42, 51
prospects, 63, 88
prudent, 88
psychographics, 22
purpose, 6, 14, 19, 27, 29, 37,
    47, 50
purposes, 50, 62, 87

Q

Quadrant of Doom, 68, 69
qualitative, 84
quantitative, 84
quicksand, 68
quit, 102

R

realist, 5, 7, 35, 56
Realtors, 43

regional, 36, 47
regulations, 23
reputation, 4
research, 67, 82, 98
resource, 6, 7, 59, 63, 65, 70, 82
resourcefulness, 58, 60, 63
responsibilities, 92
restaurants, 36
restrictions, 23
results, 2, 25, 41, 75, 87, 98,
    99, 103
retail, 46, 74
revenue, 20
rewards, 46, 98, 99
ROI, 84
Ruxton, Robert, 48

S

satisfaction, 84
Savage, Dave, 73, 74, 75, 112
scale, 27
scenarios, 32
schedule, 91
scope, 63
sector, 74
segmentation, 22, 66
selling, 41, 45, 50, 63, 64, 68,
    80, 82
sensitive, 22
shapes, 36
shareholder, 47
situation, 46, 64, 67, 69, 79,
    83, 94
Six Sigma, 99
skills, 26, 44, 46, 67, 99
SmartReply, 73
Socrates, 11
software, 43, 44, 45, 60, 69, 93

solutions, 44, 62, 69, 78
Soviet Union, 34, 96
stakeholders, 67
standards, 96
startup, 74
strategy retreat, 2, 9
strengths, 16, 29, 54, 56
stubborn, 103
subconscious, 39, 40
substitutes, 19
success, 4, 48, 54, 77, 80, 84,
    88, 89, 97, 99, 103
Sums, 14, 24
Sun Tzu, 11, 26
survey, 13
survive, 59, 69, 73, 82, 102
symptom, 31
systems, 43, 44

T

tactics, 8, 62, 64, 76, 77, 78, 86,
    87, 88, 89, 90, 91, 92, 93,
    94, 98, 99, 100, 101, 103
talent, 24, 67
tangible, 98
target, 17, 18, 20, 69
technology, 20, 29, 41, 45, 57,
    69, 97
telemarketing, 64
tenacity, 103
tension, 4, 48, 70, 71, 102
testing, 66, 88, 100
Texas, 57
Theodore, 43
theory, 14, 96
things, 9, 14, 23, 26, 32
threats, 53
timetables, 7

Titanic, 53
toothpaste, 22
traditional, 19, 46
training, 13, 46, 64, 89
transportation, 41
trends, 23, 24, 67
true, 12, 23, 28, 35, 47, 49, 76,
    82, 91, 101
turbulent, 3

U

Umpqua Bank, 46
underfunding, 88
unique, 26, 43, 44, 67, 75, 77,
    79, 83, 91, 93
United States, 61
upscale, 39
utility, 22, 42, 44

V

value, 25, 42, 47, 50, 51, 74
vertical, 57
viable, 92
victory, 6, 11, 29, 54, 78
Vietnam War, 60
vigilance, 98
Vikings, 60
vineyard, 40
vision statement, 55

W

warfare, 96
weaknesses, 16, 54, 56
webinar, 62
winning, 20, 83, 84
wisdom, 85
wise, 2, 23, 53, 70
WWII, 58

Z

Zhang Xun, 1, 2

About the **Author**

Who is Robert Stover?

Robert Stover is a business growth strategist, speaker, and writer. He's the founder of Strategy Matters, a business growth training, coaching, and consulting firm. And he has a passion for helping businesses create breakthrough growth by leveraging strategy. Over the last 24 years he's worked on marketing and strategy with companies as varied as Fortune 500 companies to startups.

He can be reached at *stover@strategymatters.com*

And you can view his blog at StrategyMatters.com